Teacher's Guide for

The Hunter Writing System

Sentence Sense

Red Level

Anthony Devereux Hunter, Sr.

Hunter & Joyce Publishing Company
Delhi, New York

THE SERIES:

THE HUNTER WRITING SYSTEM: SENTENCE SENSE, RED LEVEL
[The "red" level is the INTRODUCTORY LEVEL.]

The Hunter Writing System: Sentence Sense, Green Level
(September 1994) [The "green" level is the INTERMEDIATE LEVEL.]

At each level, there is (or will be) a consumable *Skills Practice Book* that contains all the practice material, the text itself, an *Answer Book,* and a *Teacher's Guide.*

ORDERING INFORMATION:

CALL: **607-746-3196 or 800-462-7483 (Fax: 607-746-2408)**

WRITE: **Hunter & Joyce Publishing Company**
R.R. 2, Box 54
Delhi, NY 13753

ANTHONY DEVEREUX HUNTER, SR. has taught English for twenty-nine years and Latin for one year in junior and senior high schools and in colleges in the United States. In addition, he has taught English as a second language overseas for three years. He has conducted many workshops in the area of grammar and writing. His degrees include a Ph.L. from St. Louis University and an M.A. and Ed.D.—in the teaching of high school English—from Teachers College, Columbia University.

Printed in the United States of America
ISBN: 0-9625839-2-8

Contents

Part I

Background and Helps for the Text as a Whole

The chapters in this part serve several introductory purposes. The first chapter raises and answers those questions that teachers are most likely to ask about a text that teaches writing through grammar. The second chapter gives teachers specific helps for the first day and general helps for the following days. The third gives an overview of how this text teaches the structure of a sentence. The fourth contrasts the instruction of the two levels of the text, the *Red Level* (this one) and the forthcoming *Green Level*. The fifth explains why and how the text came to be written in the first place.

Chapter 1

Answers to Questions You Might Be Asking

The goals of this *Teacher's Guide* are to give you background information about the text *The Hunter Writing System: Sentence Sense, Red Level* and to supply you with guidelines for your use of it.

Why So Short a Guide?

This text has been written so simply and directly that a boy going from 6th grade to 7th taught himself 8½ chapters and did 85-90% correct work—despite the fact that he worked a half hour at a time and would return to the task only after 5-day lapses. I was nearby to answer questions (usually a word that he did not understand and that has now been changed or clarified) and to correct his work as he requested it.

A Writing Text or a Grammar Text?

This is a writing text for many reasons. The first reason is that the "grammar" it teaches is primarily a grammar of the structure of the sentence rather than of rules or of the meanings of terms. Because its exercises require students to rearrange sentence parts and make substitutions as tests of grammatical function, they learn EXPERIENTIALLY—and, therefore, in the most meaningful way possible—the job that the grammatical parts perform. As a result, they gain a command of structure that empowers them to write more and more spontaneously, correctly, and effectively.

This is a writing text for these additional reasons. First, it provides countless models of sentences both in its examples and in its practice work. Second, its exercises include the writing of sentences in imitation of these models. Third, the very exercises that involve rearranging of sentences are themselves sometimes exercises in achieving variety and in editing. Fourth, it provides some sentence combining. Fifth, it provides instruction and practice in remedying many of the most common faults in student writing—and in such a way that the rules of usage and punctuation make sense and stick. Finally, it so steeps students in knowledge of structure and understanding of grammatical terms that all instruction based on these—that is, instruction in the rules of usage, style, mechanics, and punctuation—makes immediate sense and takes root.

In What Sense Is This Grammar Different?

This "grammar" is different because it **teaches the VERB FIRST and teaches the VERB TO MASTERY;** because it **teaches the INTERRELATIONSHIPS OF THE CHIEF COMPONENTS OF THE SENTENCE BEFORE it teaches the rest of the parts of speech and the rules of usage;** because it **uses WORKING DEFINITIONS THAT ARE ACCURATE** (rather than abstract ones that are imprecise); because it is **DISCOVERY-DRIVEN IN METHODOLOGY;** because **it uses HANDS-ON STRATEGIES that cause learning to be fresh, meaningful, and lasting;** because it teaches **VISUALLY due to its abundance of examples, graphic displays, and highlighting;** and because it **causes students to INTERNALIZE THE SYSTEM OF THE STRUCTURE of written English.**

Students internalize structure because the strategies are experience-based, because all the chief components of English are included, and because the practice work is cumulative. The effect of students' immersion in the structure of our written language is that it frees them from dependence on spoken-English patterns and enables them to **COMPOSE with greater EASE, CORRECTNESS, and DIRECTNESS and READ with greater SPEED and COMPREHENSION.**

Why Grammar at All?

There are many reasons why students need a grammar—like this one—that is true to the language and that becomes internalized due to hands-on involvement.

It helps their WRITING in these more specific ways. First, it enables students to EXPERIENCE THE NEED for correct and/or effective usage, punctuation, coherence, and variety. Second, it instills command of the word-group types in such a way that students have new-found choices in the ways they can arrange words to have the effect they want. Finally, it sensitizes students to the function of words; therefore, it causes them to choose ever more fitting words for the messages intended.

In addition, this grammar helps students' READING. To begin with, the just-mentioned sensitizing to the function of words makes it imperative that they know each word's exact meaning. Moreover, their sensitivity to word-group types enables them to pinpoint the core of the sentence without time-wasting back-tracking. Furthermore, their owning of structure enables them to read sentences according to their natural (grammatical) groupings for much faster and more accurate comprehension.

One more area in which this grammar helps students is their SPEAKING. First, it gives them command of the irregular forms of verbs. Besides that, it sensitizes them to the need for accuracy in grammar, usage, and coherence and in the development of their ideas. Lastly, it makes them owners of a wide range of ways of expressing themselves and therefore instills self-confidence.

Finally, this grammar also helps students as LISTENERS. It sensitizes them to the role of each word as it is heard. It sensitizes them to the roles of groups of words and their interrelationships, even as spoken. It makes them open to language as a vehicle to learning and comprehending, even when spoken.

Why Is This Way of Teaching Grammar Better?

There are clearly identifiable reasons why this way of teaching grammar is better. For your convenience, I have sorted them into three categories—its strategies, its exercises, and its order of arrangement.

Unique Strategies

Note these attributes of the strategies taught:

- They presuppose NO PRIOR KNOWLEDGE;
- They make THE VERB THE HUB of instruction;
- They are SIMPLE, HANDS-ON, and VERIFIABLE STRATEGIES—instead of verbal definitions of questionable merit;
- The strategies often explain the REASONS WHY ENGLISH WORKS THE WAY IT DOES.

Unique Exercises

Note these attributes of the exercises supplied:

- The exercises teach the VERB TO MASTERY;
- LATER EXERCISES DEMAND MASTERY OF EARLIER ONES (from Chapter 5 on);
- The exercises require HANDS-ON INVOLVEMENT so that structure becomes etched in memory: they entail substituting wording, rearranging of groups of words, labeling of sentence parts (as the sentence stands), and composing of sentences in imitation of models;
- They provide REINFORCEMENT OF ALL EARLIER LESSONS (in every chapter after Chapter 4 except for Chapter 12).

Unique Order of Arrangement

Note the carefully planned ordering of content:

- It teaches FIRST—AS A PRECONDITION AND FOUNDATION—HOW THE KEY PARTS OF THE SENTENCE INTERRELATE;
- It teaches THE WHOLE BEFORE THE PARTS—that is, how groups of words perform key functions before it teaches how single words perform them;
- All chapters—and lessons inside them—have SEQUENCING THAT ASSURES COMPREHENSION AND MASTERY;
- There is ONLY ONE SET OF STEPS TO GUIDE STUDENTS IN THE ANALYSIS OF SENTENCES—even the most complex ones.

At What Grade Level or Levels Does This Text Belong?

Though this text progresses in simple steps and is concrete, its grammatical content gets complex because that is the nature of a true grammar. That is why I recommend that this text be taught at the seventh grade level at earliest (certainly no earlier than sixth grade)—at least by a teacher who wishes to teach to the end of the text.

Note, however, that this text has singular importance for every youth and/or adult—regardless of grade level—whom "school grammar" has left bankrupt of command of their language's structure and of self-confidence in their use of it.

Note, finally, that there is no need to finish the whole of this text during a single school year because its sequel text, the *Green Level*, will reteach all of the lessons and build on them as it treats the still more complex elements of grammar.

Where Does Grammar Fit as a Component of Education?

It should be kept in mind that the English language has three component, self-contained systems that act as a backdrop of knowledge by means of which students are able to compose their ideas and decode the messages of others. These systems are (a) the system of the sound-spelling correspondences that prevail in English (phonics); (b) the system of the rules for decoding and creating words by means of their component parts (roots and affixes), including the spelling rules that govern the addition of prefixes and suffixes; and (c) the system of its grammar and syntax. Since grammar is the most complex of these, ideally each of the other systems should have been mastered prior to it.

Must the Chapters of the Text Be Taught in a Particular Sequence?

The answer to this is an unequivocal **YES**. Both the chapters of this text and all the lessons inside each are tightly SEQUENTIAL—that is, each new lesson presupposes not only mastery of the previous concepts but also mastery of the concepts EXACTLY AS THEY WERE

TAUGHT IN THIS TEXT. If a teacher were to bypass a lesson or chapter—or substitute a definition or explanation from some other author's vantage point—subsequent learning could be jeopardized and student success undermined. (This is especially true from Chapter 5 on.)

Such a teacher would be perpetuating one of the chief failings of school grammar—the leaving of gaps in the sequencing of instruction so that steps in the learning process are being presupposed.

How Much Time Does It Take to Teach This Text?

Assuming that a teacher intends to teach the whole of the text (which is not a necessity—as just indicated), he/she would need to spend ten to twelve weeks with it for an average seventh or eighth grade class. This timing guideline presupposes that there would be regular take-home assignments and that a moderate number of composition assignments (not built into the text as it now stands) would also be part of these two to three months of work. Note that the simultaneous composition work (which can be of any kind) concretizes for students the interconnections between their increasing insights into sentence structure and the ways they express themselves.

Note, too, that there are ways in which you can achieve the goals of the text—especially the chief ones—in a shorter time. See the section "Recommendations for Reducing Instruction Time" on pages 12 and 13 of this *Guide*.

For an average ninth grade (or higher) class, the instruction time would take approximately eight to ten weeks under comparable circumstances.

Note that whenever the text provides two exercises of equal difficulty, some students may omit the second one without harm. In general, high-ability students may gain adequate mastery of content by completing from one half to two thirds of the exercise material.

Is the Text Appropriate for Second-language Learners of English?

It is the experience of the author and others that second-language learners of English benefit immensely from this instruction. Students from Hong Kong, China, Africa, Haiti, the Dominican Republic, as well as other countries have all done extremely well with it. The reason is that the text offers countless examples and such continual repetition (in the cumulative exercise material) that these students learn by induction, if not by deduction. Moreover, the oral repetition of the sentences—as the answers are worked out before students' eyes—adds the benefit of spoken reinforcement of the grammatical components that are being taught (consequently, intonation is being learned as well).

Can You Give Examples of Success from Use of This Instruction?

I chanced to meet a former (college-level) student of mine two years after he had taken my course. He reported that he had just spent a summer as supervisor of several work sites for a construction company. He said that it was only because of the training that I had given him in grammar that he had been able to handle the battery of important communication activities that his job entailed—letter writing, phoning, and hiring and firing. In fact, I met him because he had become a member of our faculty, an instructor in one of the Vocational Education programs that trained students for managerial positions in the field of construction.

Another student who greatly benefited from the grammar was a girl in our Veterinary Science program, one of our most difficult programs. She said that she used to have to read material three times to understand it but that her learning of grammar now enabled her to understand what she read at the FIRST reading.

In my public speaking classes, it was INVARIABLY true that the students to whom I had taught Freshman English (and, therefore, my grammar work) were competent at extemporaneous speaking—they spoke intelligibly and effectively when they ad-libbed. In contrast, MORE THAN HALF of the other students, who had also taken Freshman English but without emphasis on a grammar that teaches how the structure of English works, were UNABLE to express themselves either intelligibly or effectively when trying to speak extemporaneously.

Another student of mine, who worked hard but had not stood out especially in my class, was amazed when her teacher in the sequel (Advanced Composition) course held her writing up as a model of effective prose.

In anonymous questionnaires at the end of Freshman English and developmental/remedial writing courses, I would question students as to how helpful different components of the course had been for their writing and reading. Up to 80% responded that the grammar component had been either "of much help" or "of very much help" for their WRITING (vs. "of some help" or "of no help"). In addition, up to 75% responded that grammar had been of "much" or of "very much" help for their READING.

What Do Students Say about This Instruction?

Students at the college level made several striking comments. More than one exclaimed, "Why didn't anyone tell me this before?" Several said that I was the first teacher they had had who explained why English works the way it does. Some students—in the middle of instruction on the verb (and after some work with word parts and spelling rules)—said that they had already learned more English than in all of the twelve years that had preceded.

At the middle school level, too, students have given this work uncommon endorsement. One teacher reported that her students said that the work was fun and "like a game, like Nintendo." Another teacher reported that her students had "accepted the program enthusiastically" and were "anxious to master grammar, something that many of them [had] been unsuccessful at for several years." Students have written that they were "looking forward to the next lesson."

What Do Teachers Say about This Instruction?

A teacher who has taught three sections of seventh graders through Chapter 10 reports that "the system does work" and that her "students were pleased to have a true system" rather than a by-guess-and-by-golly one. She has also reported that she has had success in helping students understand complete sentences and run-ons due to the chapters on verbs, subjects, and predicates. She wrote, "It [teaching your text] did make a difference in last year's students' writing."

A teacher who has taught three sections of ninth graders to almost the end of (the current) Chapter 7 made several comments. She had yet to hit a snag. She felt that the text was clearly written and easy to understand. She appreciated the number of practice exercises provided for each new concept because this exposed her students to a variety of situations in which the new concept might appear. She felt that this new approach allowed her students a fresh start with grammar, one not laden with grammatical terms and definitions right from the beginning. Finally, she said:

> I believe this program is easily adaptable to a variety of classroom situations. The style lends itself to independent study or group work. And because prior knowl-

edge is not required in the way of terms and definitions, this program can be introduced at almost any grade level. I am excited to be involved in this program....

What Has an English Educator Said about This Instruction?

After he was introduced to how this way of teaching grammar works, Richard L. Knudson, a professor of English Education at the State University of New York in Oneonta, had two reactions. One was, "This is fun." The other was that these methods would work with any sentence in English, not just with the ones in the book.

Why Two Books and Not One?

My text causes learning primarily through the type of exercises it provides. These exercises require students to add labeling to the words in sentences to indicate their mastery of the techniques of the text. If the numberless exercises of the text all had to be copied before students could carry them out, it would be a miscarriage of education.

How Does This Grammar Relate to the Whole Language Approach?

This text is a whole-language approach to teaching grammar for at least two reasons. First, its goal and effects are the simultaneous improvement of writing, reading, speaking, and listening. Second, it satisfies students' innate curiosity as to why their language works the way it does; it is self-motivating.

In addition, it provides an indispensable foundation for whole-language learning because it embeds in students' minds the SYSTEM of the structure of the sentence. ONLY FROM SUCH A POINT OF REFERENCE can instruction pertaining to improvement of style, usage, punctuation, and reading take firm root and be lasting.

How Does This Grammar Relate to the Process Approach to Teaching Writing?

Just as this text is the foundation for the whole-language approach, similarly it is the foundation for the process approach. If the work of this text precedes or accompanies students' composition efforts, **they will compose MUCH MORE** and **compose MUCH MORE QUICKLY** because they will have control of sentence structure. In addition, they will **compose WORK OF MUCH HIGHER QUALITY** because of their sensitivity to the interrelationships of meaning, structure, and punctuation (they will be their own editors).

Note that the process approach to teaching writing advocates the use of occasional "mini-workshops" to teach lessons in grammar. It is my conviction that mastery of the SYSTEM OF THE STRUCTURE OF ENGLISH requires far more extensive and systematic instruction regarding the way our language works and far more practice time than the format of an occasional mini-workshop permits; it requires the kind of systematic instruction and cumulative practice that this text furnishes.

Isn't Grammar More Meaningful When Taught in the Context of a Student's Own Writing?

The answer is NO. Grammar—to be meaningful—must be taught inside the set of truths that make up the system of the structure of our language. These truths are the ones that govern the positions of words and their endings and that control the functions of words when given these positions or endings; they are the truths that empower writers, consciously or subconsciously, to carve their thoughts in words easily, correctly, and tellingly.

The truths that make up this system are far too many and complex to be mastered in random order and/or OUTSIDE A CLOSELY CONTROLLED STRUCTURAL FRAME OF REFERENCE—no matter how meaningful the verbal context is in the mind of a writer. The only way to master these truths is through a text, like this, that implants the truths in a meaningful and carefully controlled STRUCTURAL context so that comprehension, assimilation, and retention—at the structural level—are assured.

Why Not Save Grammar Until Students' Minds Are More Mature?

Operationally, students have mastered the intricacies of the grammar of their SPOKEN language from early childhood.

Since the "grammar" in this text capitalizes on this base of experiential knowledge, it can be taught at almost any grade level.

Nonetheless, I have chosen to introduce it at the seventh grade level for several reasons. First, its final chapters handle elements of grammar of such complexity that most children who are younger than seventh graders would struggle with it. Second, it is in seventh grade, by and large, that students from various elementary schools set out afresh together. Third, it is more common that at the seventh grade level, teachers of English are trained as specialists in language arts rather than as "generalists." Finally, it is in seventh and eighth grades that schools are beginning to offer a second period of the day for mastery of language arts; this added time would be perfect for the introduction of this text, which is so important a foundation not only for the learning of the rest of language arts but also for becoming learners of any subject matter.

Is This Text Suitable for Use at the High School, College, and Adult Levels?

The answer is YES. First, it has the same content as the text that I used when teaching Freshman English to college students. Second, it is easy enough to read that at these levels it could be self-teaching. Finally, its exercises have universal appeal.

Moreover, all students—at whatever age—who have been disserved by school grammar's failure to give them control of our language's structure will remain deficient in their command of English without a grammar like this to empower them.

Chapter 2

What to Do on Day 1 and Other Recommendations

What to Do on Day 1

Grouping and Timing

This is a straightforward text. You can teach it to a whole class at once (no special grouping is necessary). You start with page 1 of Chapter 1 and teach the pages consecutively. **(If you lack time to teach this text as thoroughly as recommended here, you will find several helps for teaching the text in less time explained at the end of this chapter. See the section entitled "Recommendations for Reducing Instruction Time" on pages 12 and 13. Note, however, that almost all of the tips and guidelines of this chapter will still have relevance.)** A day's instruction can take an entire class period or part of a period, according to the pace you choose. Throughout the text, the instruction lends itself to your giving assignments to be done outside of class.

Teaching Strategy

In terms of classroom strategy, you can turn the frequent headings into questions and then explain the content—ideally in your own words and with your own examples—IN THE SAME WAY AS IN THE TEXT. You then test their understanding by having them do the practice work that has been provided. (Look for the large black dot [●] that signals the presence of each exercise.) I recommend—as part of every assignment—that you FIRST have students read over the relevant pages of the text and THEN do the practice work assigned.

Chapters 1–4 vs. Chapter 5 to the End

Note that Chapters 1–4 have a much different purpose than the remaining chapters. In these beginning chapters, the sole intent is to familiarize students with the terms and in such a way as to give them just the background they need to complete the rest of the text without gaps in their understanding. The goal is NOT mastery but an experience-based ACQUAINTANCE. The only practice they need is what is provided with the text; a word-by-word recall of definitions would NOT be expected or even beneficial. On the other hand, they should be able to give you an example of the important terms when you ask for one. Note that most of the content of Chapters 1–4 is taken up again in later chapters and with the expectation—only then—of mastery.

Chapter 5 to End

From Chapter 5 on (with the exception only of Chapter 12), mastery of instruction is a requirement. For this reason, students must maintain close to a 90% average to be adequately prepared for subsequent lessons; and retention of the rules and of the meanings of terms—at least in students' own wording—is also a requirement.

Because mastery is so important, I strongly recommend that you give students as much time and practice as they need to achieve this. It is better for students to learn the chapters and their lessons in sequence and NOT finish the book than for them to finish the text but not have effectively absorbed much of anything. This is true not only because later chapters cannot be mastered without mastery of what preceded but also because every chapter of the text has the built-in reward for students of their having advanced one more notch in their understanding of the way in which English really works.

Evaluation

Note that evaluation of student success is easy. You can judge that by how well they do with the practice work. In addition, from Chapter 5 on (but not Chapter 12), exercises usually come in pairs—and later exercises are cumulative—so that you could use either of a pair as a "quiz" or "test." Finally, you can gauge success at the end of each chapter by using the tests provided at the end of each chapter in Part II of this *Guide*.

Other General Recommendations

Here are some general recommendations:

✓ **START TEACHING THE TEXT AS CLOSE TO THE START OF THE SCHOOL YEAR AS POSSIBLE.** This will enable your students to absorb more, and therefore benefit more, from all the instruction that follows it.

✓ **FAMILIARIZE YOURSELF WITH THE DETAILS OF THE WHOLE TEXT BEFORE YOU TEACH THE FIRST LESSON.** This will give you a personal awareness of the purpose of each chapter as you teach it.

✓ **INTERNALIZE THE CONTENT OF EACH LESSON BEFORE TEACHING IT.** You can do this best by doing a few of EACH of the practices of a chapter so you can experience in advance what the text is trying to do for students.

✓ **EXPECT YOUR STUDENTS TO SUCCEED.** To them, it will be exciting and refreshing because this is a "grammar" that makes sense to them.

✓ **BE AWARE OF THE SINGLE-FOCUS NATURE OF MOST OF THE EXERCISES.** Because students are expected to find only one component at a time, they can concentrate on just the job at hand and be more sure to succeed.

✓ **EXPLAIN TO YOUR STUDENTS THAT THIS IS A SYSTEM THAT MAKES SENSE AND WORKS if they should object that it is different from what they have been taught.** Explain that it will give them insights into our language and power in their use of it that school grammar strategies are unable to furnish—that it teaches the verb to mastery and then uses the verb as a springboard to teach how the key components of the sentence work together to form the nucleus of the sentence and serve as an anchor for all the other parts of structure.

✓ **DO NOT LET STUDENTS RELY ON STRATEGIES THAT ARE UNRELATED TO THE EXPLANATIONS IN THE TEXT.** The reason for this is that later lessons depend not only on mastery of preceding content but also on mastery of previously taught strategies.

✓ **SHOW STUDENTS WHAT THE ANSWERS LOOK LIKE—ideally on an overhead projector—as you work through with them how you and they arrive at them.** This causes reinforcement of learning—and through more than one of their senses.

✓ **ADAPTATION OF THE TEXT FOR THE USE OF MORE ADVANCED STUDENTS involves assigning the completion of a PORTION of each exercise (versus all or most of**

each). You may also want to adopt some of the strategies for going quicker that are listed in the last section of this chapter.

✓ **ADAPTATION OF THE TEXT FOR USE WITH BELOW-AVERAGE STUDENTS would require that you give the learning all the time it needs.** You would probably need to assign all the exercise material, go over all the answers before their eyes, and quiz and test more frequently to assure remembering of strategies.

✓ **ADAPTATION OF THE TEXT FOR USE WITH AVERAGE STUDENTS would require a blend of the suggestions just given.** Adjust the timing, the use of visual display of answers, the amount of discussion of exercise answers, and the amount of quizzing and testing according to the needs of the students. Start early in the semester; give them all the time that they need; make the instruction as continuous as possible—that is, with as few intervening days without this kind of instruction as possible; and prefer a slower pace WITH mastery to a faster pace without it. Let any left-over chapters be taken up in a following year—but only after a review of the previous year's instruction (that has been accompanied by sufficient practice) has taken place as a foundation.

✓ **THE SHADED MATERIAL IS MATERIAL THAT STUDENTS MUST KEEP REMEMBERED—preferably in their own words** (from Chapter 5 on especially).

✓ **Note that the appendix on the RULES FOR AGREEMENT OF A VERB WITH ITS SUBJECT should be taught after Chapter 15 and not before it.** This is because it presupposes the instruction of Chapter 15 for a number of the rules.

✓ **STUDENTS SHOULD DEVISE A WAY TO KEEP THE MOST IMPORTANT PARTS OF THE TEXT REMEMBERED—ESPECIALLY THE STEPS AND THEIR ORDER INSIDE THE "TESTS."** They must not forget this content. **PERIODICAL AND CUMULATIVE TESTING OF THEIR KNOWLEDGE OF ALL SUCH MEMORY** (not included in the end-of-chapter tests here) **WOULD GREATLY HELP THEM.**

✓ **IF ONE OF THE END-OF-CHAPTER FINAL TESTS PROVIDED IN THIS *GUIDE* IS TOO LONG OR TOO SHORT, ADAPT IT TO SUIT YOUR STUDENTS' NEEDS.**

Recommendations of a Current Teacher

1. "Fight the urge to teach everything at once—and therefore prematurely."
2. "Buy into this approach 100%. Begin completely new. Though the patterns of learning (the terms and approach) are different, the approach is very successful and kids are very receptive."
3. "Do not bring in outside information. That will dilute the content and distract the students."
4. "Note that the text's goals (and yours as its teacher) are to give students a better understanding of language and how it works and not just definitions to know. Its goal is to have them understand the patterns of wording by manipulating sentences successfully and NOT to have them analyze the parts of speech. This is a discovery method of learning; and students do learn the parts of speech BUT BY MEANS OF THE PROCESS."

Recommendations for Reducing Instruction Time

For those who must achieve the goals of the text in less time, there are five strategies that may make this possible. These are as follows: **reduce the content to just the grammatical core; teach background material only at the point of immediate relevance; reduce the amount of practice material assigned; and shorten the amount of class time spent on the correction of assignments.** Each of these strategies will be addressed in the subsections that follow.

Reduce the content. You could limit your teaching to only those parts of the text that contain the grammatical core. You will have achieved this if you prepare your students to score approximately 90% or better on the final tests for Chapters 1, 2, 4–11, and 13–17 that have been provided at the end of the respective chapters in Part II of this *Guide.* Note that the effects of this are to eliminate some introductory matter that gets fuller treatment at a later stage of the text, to bypass instruction on the rules of usage and punctuation, and to omit simultaneous composition work.

Teach background material only at the point of immediate relevance. For example, one or more "truths" that introduce material to come somewhat later in a chapter could be taught more briefly (say, by way simply of examples) if taught only at the point of immediate relevance.

Reduce the amount of practice material assigned. You can reduce the amount of practice work assigned either by assigning a portion (say one half) of every practice or by assigning only one of two practices when the two are alike in difficulty and purpose.

This is always a way to save time (though less advisable a way for underachievers) PROVIDED THAT YOU TEACH THE TEXT ON CONSECUTIVE DAYS. The reason why consecutive teaching allows the reduction of practice work is that, throughout the text (except in Chapters 1–4 and 12), the practice work for a new lesson requires the prior carrying out of EVERYTHING ALREADY LEARNED. For this reason, every exercise of every chapter contains reinforcement of earlier learning; and the cumulative exercises contain reinforcement of virtually all previous learning.

There are two formats for teaching the text that especially lend themselves to consecutive instruction. One would be to devote at least TEN MINUTES A DAY TO THE TEXT ALL YEAR LONG (five minutes would be for instruction and five minutes for correction of approximately twenty minutes worth of assigned practice material). The other format would be to dedicate A BLOCK OF TIME, SUCH AS SIX WEEKS, to the teaching of this material alone.

Have students do more of the practices outside of class. You will often want students to START assignments in class so you can be sure that they have understood everything. However, the more practice work that they do outside of class, the more class time remains for correcting earlier work and/or proceeding faster.

Shorten the amount of class time spent on the correction of assignments. There are several ways in which you can get the correcting of student work done faster (though rarely so effectively as working at least some of them out before their eyes as on an overhead projector).

First, you could show them the answers ALREADY WORKED OUT on an overhead projector (they could correct their own work or one another's as you do this). Second, you could DUPLICATE ANSWERS and hand them out (again, they could correct their own work or one another's). Third, you could collect their books, correct their work in your free time, and then have them pick up their books in time to do the next assignment. Fourth, if your students are capable of this, you could have them correct each other's work; and you would then become the arbiter in cases of disagreements.

There is one precaution to keep in mind. You should not be so hurried that you fail to make sure that each student has understood any mistake made.

Chapter 3

An Overview of the System

My attempt in this chapter is to give you an overview of the "system of grammar" that is the heart of this text. I will list, in the briefest possible way, those steps that give students control over the sentence's structure. (Note that if you find this chapter difficult to understand—because it is so concentrated—do not let it bother you. The text itself provides a simpler explanation and presents it at a far more "user-friendly" pace.)

In Chapters 5-7 (Chapters 1–4 are introductory), the text teaches two valid ways of finding those verbs that stand at the center of sentences and/or clauses. By the end of Chapter 7, students know all the helping verbs on sight and can find verb phrases accurately; in addition, they can change verbs like *wanted* to their alternative form *did want*.

In Chapters 9 and 10, they learn how to convert statements to questions by shifting the one helping verb that "works" to the front of the sentence. For example, they would change the sentence *My brother from Texas could have arrived on time* to:

[COULD] My brother from Texas ... have arrived on time?

This conversion serves two purposes. First, the helping verb that shifts like this MUST BELONG TO the verb that makes the sentence a sentence—here called the "core verb." Second, the wording between the two positions of the helping verb that shifts MUST BE the subject of that verb—here called the "main subject." This core verb and its subject are the core of the sentence (they make up the "main clause").

In Chapter 11, the text teaches students to notice that many sentences in English do NOT begin with the core of the sentence. Instead, they begin with wording that the author could alternatively have placed at the end of the sentence. Because this wording usually has a COMMA after it, students learn to take notice of commas and to test whether they can shift wording that they find before a comma to the end of the sentence.

For example, when students see a sentence such as *If he had left earlier, my brother from Texas could have arrived on time*, they reword it in this way:

my brother from Texas could have arrived on time IF HE HAD LEFT EARLIER

Students learn that front wording that can shift like this must be kept COVERED while they test for the helping verb that shifts because that helping verb can only shift to where the front wording has ended. (They also learn where commas belong and how to add variety to their sentences.)

Note that they learn to apply comparable strategies to questions in Chapters 8 and 13.

With mastery of these core units of the sentence as a foundation, students can quickly master the roles of nouns (and their replacers) in the SUBJECT, OBJECT OF VERB and OBJECT OF PREPOSITION territories.

They then look for adjectives primarily INSIDE one of these noun territories; and they look for all adverbs (except those that modify adjectives) OUTSIDE such noun territories.

They locate dependent clauses easily because these have as their anchor those verbs that are "left over" after the core verb has been found.

Notice how complete accuracy in identification of the verb is of utmost importance in this way of teaching how English works.

Chapter 4

The Red and Green Levels Compared

The texts at the *Red* and *Green Levels* are complementary in the sense that the *Green Level* of the text reteaches everything that is in the *Red Level* and builds on it.

The Red Level

The text's *Red Level* is INTRODUCTORY in the sense that its goal is to teach only those elements of the structure of English that are most needed to give students control over their writing and reading.

This focusing on only the most important components prevents students from getting discouraged either by too much detail or by content of too great difficulty and from getting distracted from what is truly important. Though they learn all the parts of speech in depth (except the interjection), they learn about the more sophisticated and less immediately important predicate noun and adjective, indirect object, noun in apposition, and verbal phrase only in passing. Note that the text does introduce students to dependent clauses at this level because these are so centrally important a component of our language.

The Green Level

The text's *Green Level* is INTERMEDIATE in difficulty. First, though it reteaches the content of the *Red Level* text, it does so with fewer exercises. Second, it teaches the more sophisticated and complex elements of English that were only mentioned in passing or omitted in the *Red Level* work. It teaches the following: predicate nouns, indirect objects, nouns in apposition, and predicate adjectives in depth; dependent clauses in greater depth; parenthetical expressions; compound elements in greater depth; and infinitive, participial, and gerund phrases in some depth.

How Much Instruction in This "Grammar" Would Be Ideal

Students should have a minimum of two "years" of instruction in this way of learning the structure of our language. A third "year" of such instruction would be even better. (For above-average students, the third "year" might be a review of the contents of the text with only limited emphasis on carrying out exercises.) The purpose of the overlapping of instruction is to permanently imprint in students' minds the experience-based knowledge of terms and internalization of structure that are the fruits of the exercises of the text.

Chapter 5

Why and How This Text Came to Be Written

This chapter spells out those aspects of my background that especially equipped and motivated me to write this text.

There are two components of my education that have been singularly helpful. One of these is my extensive training in languages, not only in French but also, and especially, in Latin and Greek. The other component is my postgraduate work for two years in philosophy (my Ph.L. or "Licentiate to Teach Philosophy" degree). This work trained me to be an innovative thinker.

An experience that greatly influenced the starting of this work and enabled some of its insights was the three years that I spent teaching English to "high schoolers" in the Philippine Islands. Because the texts available were too difficult for these students, I began creating my own grammar text. That text caused dramatic improvement especially in the reading ability of my students but also in their writing. As a result, I was strongly encouraged as an author and innovator.

Also when I was in the Philippines, I started to learn two of the dialects of the country, Bicol and Tagalog. The insights into language that I gained from the contrast between these Austronesian languages and English gave me a unique vantage point from which to analyze how English works.

I then started teaching on Long Island at a school where my assignment was to teach just grammar and spelling to seventh grade students. As you might have guessed, the text that I used was one that I was creating from day to day as I taught. It was during my three years at this school that I arrived at my best insights into how English works.

After this, I went on to earn a Doctor of Education degree in the teaching of English at Teachers College, Columbia University. It was there that I had the good fortune to work under the linguist Robert L. Allen, who was also head of my doctoral committee. He insisted that I incorporate his "sector analysis," the name that he gave to his linguistic theory, into the work that I had already done. For my doctoral dissertation, I arranged a field testing of the resultant text. There were five teachers involved besides myself. Their recommendations were incorporated into the published version of that text—which is an ancestor of this one.

When I started teaching at the State University of New York at Delhi, I came to realize that the text needed two improvements. It needed closer adherence to traditional terminology and more applications to writing (the text that had been field tested had been designed primarily as a reading text).

As I taught the evolving material over the semesters, I kept improving it and expanding it. This repeated field testing enabled me to improve the order of instruction and to supply any missing links in the chain of concepts. There were over a thousand students who received this instruction.

Prior to publication, several junior high school teachers piloted the final version that had been developed at the college level. Their recommendations have been incorporated in the text as you now see it.

The final stage in the development of the text was its adaptation from a text written for college students to a text readable and usable by junior high school students (even as young as seventh graders) and high school students. All the old wording was abandoned; every heading was rethought; charts and shading were added; the exercises were changed and expanded; and some content was added—all to meet the needs of a less prepared audience. This phase took an entire twelve months.

Since publication, the text has been piloted at the seventh and eighth grade levels with success and commendation.

Part II

Chapter-by-chapter Helps

The numbering of these chapters coincides with the numbering of the chapters in the text at the *Red Level.* Chapter by chapter, they provide the following: the chapter's objectives, teaching helps, a final test, answers to the test, and weights for scoring the final test.

Note: Throughout these chapters, page references will be indicated as follows: to the text [Text, x]; to the *Skills Practice Book* [Skills, x]—where "x" stands for a particular page number.

Chapter 1

Background for Understanding Verbs

Objectives (Items in bolder letters are of greatest importance)

TO **INTRODUCE ONLY** THESE TERMS:

- **Main verb** (with practice)
- **Helping verb** (with practice)
- **Names for the two kinds of helping verbs—starters and followers**
- **Verb phrase**
- **Names for the components (spellings) of a verb—basic, S, ING, past tense, and after-had**
- Sentence (with practice)
- Dependent clause (with practice)
- Importance (roles) of verb
- Job of verb
- Subject
- Tense (present, past, future)
- Regular vs. irregular verb

Teaching Helps

TEACHING SUGGESTIONS

Writing of sentences: Note that I do not ask students to write sentences of their own here. This is because I do not ask this of them until they have better control of the ingredients that make up the type of sentence that I wish them to imitate.

Additional practice: It would be ill-advised to give students more practice than the text offers here. The mastery instruction has not begun yet.

ALTERNATIVE "EXAMPLES"

If you use your own wording to introduce a section of the text to your students—and I recommend this—you should PARAPHRASE THE WORDING OF THE TEXT'S EXAMPLES as much as possible, especially in these beginning chapters. Wherever I feel that it would be helpful, I supply alternative examples for you in this *Guide*. I will do this by citing the page number where the heading is, and by repeating the heading and the wording of the example so you will know the exact place in the text.

PAGES	HEADING	EXAMPLES AS IN BOOK	ALTERNATIVE EXAMPLES
2	Sentence	*Has Ed arrived?* *A truck is coming.* *Drive carefully.*	***Did Carlos leave?*** ***A letter has fallen.*** ***Listen well.***
2–3	Dependent Clause	*if Ed has arrived* *Everyone is here if Ed has arriv-ed.*	***if the garage is open*** ***They have returned if the garage is open.***
4–5	Tense	*Beth understands. / We under-stand.* *Everyone understood.* *Everyone will understand.*	***Time flies. / Minutes fly.*** ***Time flew.*** ***Time will fly.***
8	Length of Verb Phrases	*Al will carry everything.* *Al will have carried everything.* *Bags will have been carried aboard.* *The Olympic torch will have been being carried uninterrupt-edly for an entire week.*	***We will study everything.*** ***We will have studied every-thing.*** ***Our books could have been brought home.*** ***Our studying for that test should not have been be-ing done while watching TV.***
9–10	Components of Main Verbs	*break / breaks / breaking / broke / broken*	***freeze/freezes/freezing/froze/ frozen***
10	Jobs of Com-ponents	*agree / will agree*	***see / will see***
10	Names for the Five Compo-nents	*break vs. want*	***freeze vs. last***
12–13	Starters as Main Verbs	*Everyone did well.* *Bill has enough money.* *Maria is the captain.*	***We do our best.*** ***No one had a quarter.*** ***The box is full.***
13	Followers as Main Verbs	*We should have more scrap paper.* *Three pages will be enough.* *Joanne has been captain for two years.*	***We may have a thermos.*** ***The task will be easy.*** ***Everyone has been helpful.***

COMMENTS ON THE "ENDNOTES" SECTION [Text, 12–13]

The content in the "Endnote" sections of the text is sometimes just for background information.

The definition of the verb [Text, 13] is such an endnote. It has been included solely for the sake of completeness. I recommend that you do NOT even mention it in your teaching.

In contrast, the DISCUSSIONS OF STARTERS AND FOLLOWERS AS MAIN VERBS HAVE THE PURPOSE OF PREVENTING A MISCONCEPTION;

that content will be taught to mastery in Chapter 6 AND SHOULD BE MENTIONED HERE.

COMMENT ON THE "REVIEW" SECTION [Text, 13–14]

Do **not** take the wording in the book "definitions in darker lettering must be remembered" literally for this chapter.

All that students need to "remember" is what the text and practices teach them—namely: that the main verb is the last word in a verb phrase or a stand-alone verb; that helping verbs are the verb word(s) before a main verb; that the two kinds of helping verbs have the names starters and followers; and that there are five components/spellings for a verb with the names (in this text) of basic, S, ING, past tense, and after-had spellings.

Besides this, they should be able to give the right name to a verb phrase and each of the words inside one. In addition, they should be able to write out five spellings for an irregular verb like *see* or *swim* and give the text's name for each of the spellings.

FINAL TEST

1. WRITE OUT THE FIVE SPELLINGS FOR THE VERB *FREEZE*. Use *five* lines.
2. *Beside each of the spellings that you gave in your first answer*, WRITE OUT THE CORRECT NAME FOR EACH SPELLING.
3. WRITE OUT THE ONE NAME FOR THIS GROUP OF VERB WORDS: ***HAS BEEN TALKING***.
4. WRITE OUT THE THREE NAMES FOR THE THREE VERB WORDS ***HAS, BEEN,*** and ***TALKING***. First, write the verb word; then, beside it, write the name that belongs to it as part of the group.

ANSWERS FOR THE FINAL TEST

1. *freeze / freezes / freezing / froze / frozen*
2. *freeze*=BASIC SPELLING / *freezes=S* SPELLING / *freezing=ING* SPELLING / *froze*=PAST TENSE SPELLING / *frozen*=AFTER-HAD SPELLING
3. *has been talking*=VERB PHRASE
4. *has*=STARTER / *been*=FOLLOWER / *talking*=MAIN VERB

POSSIBLE WEIGHTING OF ANSWERS FOR THE FINAL TEST

1. Each answer is worth 5% (=25%).
2. Each answer is worth 7% (=35%).
3. The answer is worth 10% (=10%).
4. Each answer is worth 10% (=30%).

Chapter 2

Nouns and Their Replacers

Objectives (Items in bolder letters are of greatest importance)

TO INTRODUCE ONLY THESE TERMS/ITEMS:

- **Noun** (with practice)
- **Proper noun** (with practice)
- **Pronouns**—also **personal, indefinite,** and demonstrative pronouns (with practice)
- Noun cluster
- Article
- Subject, as noun job
- Object of verb, as noun job
- Object of preposition, as noun job
- Preposition
- Noun Replacer
- Phrase that does the job of a noun
- Noun clause
- Names for the spellings (components) of a personal pronoun—as subject, object, adjective, indicator of ownership, and indicator of self (with practice)
- The THE Test to Find Nouns
- The Capital Letter Test to Find Nouns

Teaching Helps

COMMENTS ON THE *SKILLS PRACTICE BOOK* AND *ANSWER BOOK*

Practices E–M: In Practices E through M [Skills, 8–11] (with the exception of Practice J), there are many words that would be pronouns except for the fact that they FUNCTION AS ADJECTIVES—that is, they stand before nouns that you can say them with. Similarly, the word *most,* in Practice K [Skills, 10, next-to-last sentence], also functions as an adjective; you can say *"most types."*

TEACHING SUGGESTION

Additional practice: It would be ill-advised to give students more practice than the text offers here. The mastery instruction has not begun yet.

POINT TO BE NOTED

Demonstrative Pronouns [Text, 29–30]: The word *THAT* has several uses in English, only one of which is its use as a demonstrative pronoun. It can introduce dependent clauses (both as subordinating conjunction and relative pronoun) and can do the jobs of adjective and adverb as well. Note that the exercises of the text are controlled so that students will not see the word *that* used in these other ways until they are prepared to handle them.

ALTERNATIVE "EXAMPLES"

Again, here is alternative wording for some of the example material in the text. It can help you introduce the material in a way that is different from the book's.

PAGES	HEADING	EXAMPLES AS IN BOOK	ALTERNATIVE EXAMPLES
15	Nouns	*A horse is an animal that will obey its owner.*	***The glass of juice on the table is only partly full.***
16-17	The Job of the Subject	*Trees sway.* *Ice melts.* *Echoes reverberate.*	***Flowers bloom.*** ***Night fades.*** ***Cookies disappear.***
17-18	Three Noun Jobs	*Sunshine has warmth.* *Jan came with friends.*	***Friendliness invites friendship.*** ***We swam with flippers.***
18	Diagram ... Noun Jobs	*Librarians place books on shelves.*	***Dogs chase balls with delight.***
19-20	Proper Nouns	*One of the theaters in New York City is Radio City Music Hall.* *Mr. friend Jim Baxter lives in Dallas, Texas.* *Dorothy Hamill skates.* *General Motors Company thrives.*	***In Seattle, you can see Mount Rainier and the Olympic Mountain Range.*** ***Sam Walton, the billionaire, was born in Kingfisher, Oklahoma.*** ***AT&T advertises.*** **Wheel of Fortune *entertains.***
21	Noun Clusters	*The rather old tree has lost a diseased limb.* *The oldest boy works.* *Well-prepared students excel.*	***A rather bright painting decorates our hall.*** ***An all-blue bird exists.*** ***High-flying hawks soar.***
22	Pronouns	*The boy beside me said that he had placed his beside mine.*	***The person behind us said that he had put his beside ours.***
23	As Subjects	*We are on one side, but they are on the other.*	***She is on the sunny side, and he is in the shade.***
24	As Objects	*Mary took them with her.*	***Our parents took us with them.***
25	As Adjectives	*Their horse won his first race with its purse.* *Their plans changed.*	***Our neighbor bought her first cat and its litter.*** ***His chances improved.***
25	Indicators of Ownership	*His is with mine, but yours is on the chair.*	***His stayed with yours, but ours are with us.***
26	Indicators of "Self"	*George could picture himself as a catcher.*	***Marge could not imagine herself as a soldier.***

PAGES	HEADING	EXAMPLES AS IN BOOK	ALTERNATIVE EXAMPLES
27	**Indefinite Pronouns**	*Someone with nothing cannot easily impress anybody.*	***Somebody with nothing should not pretend to have anything.***
29	**Demonstrative Pronouns**	*This is my hat; that is yours; and those are theirs.*	***Those are their supplies; this is mine; and these are yours.***
30	**Phrases That Do Noun Jobs**	*To catch fish is fun.* *Catching fish is fun.*	***To win a race is exciting.*** ***Winning a race is exciting.***
30-31	**Noun Clauses**	*When we should leave has not been decided.* *Everyone wondered how the gadget worked.*	***When we might leave is being discussed.*** ***No one knew when the bus would arrive.***

COMMENT ON THE "REVIEW" SECTION [Text, 31–33]

Do **not** take the wording in the book "definitions in darker lettering must be remembered" literally for this chapter either.

All that students need to "remember" is what the text and practices teach them—namely: how to find nouns by means of both the THE Test and the Capital Letter Test, all the personal pronouns in their basic spelling, and a few indefinite pronouns. Besides this, they should know that nouns have territories to which they belong, that the job of a pronoun is to replace a noun, and that pronouns come in family-like groups.

FINAL TEST

1. WRITE THE LETTER N OVER ALL THE NOUNS IN THIS PASSAGE. Use both the THE Test and the Capital Letter Test.

   On his trip from Troy, Michigan, my brother traveled through Canada, picked up his sister at LeMoyne College in Syracuse, left a friend off in Cortland, and took Route 206 from Whitney Point to get to Bainbridge.

2. List the SEVEN (BASIC) PERSONAL PRONOUNS.

3. List any THREE INDEFINITE PRONOUNS.

ANSWERS FOR THE FINAL TEST

1. On his trip(N) from Troy(N), Michigan(N), my brother(N) traveled through Canada(N), picked up his sister(N) at LeMoyne College(N) in Syracuse(N), left a friend(N) off in Cortland(N), and took Route 206(N) from Whitney Point(N) to get to Bainbridge(N).

2. *you, he, it, she, they, I, we*

3. *anyone, anything, anybody*

POSSIBLE WEIGHTING OF ANSWERS FOR THE FINAL TEST

1. Each answer is worth 4% (=52%).
2. Each answer is worth 5% (=35%).
3. Each answer is worth 5% (=15%).

Chapter 3

Introduction to Agreement of Verbs with Their Subjects

Objectives (Items in bolder letters are of greatest importance)

TO **LEARN TO REMEMBER** THESE TERMS/ITEMS:

- **Number (singular, plural)** (with practice)
- **Person (first, second, third)** (with practice)
- **Agreement in number** (with practice)
- **Agreement in person** (with practice)

TO BE ABLE TO EXECUTE:

- **Changes (spellings) for a verb in its present tense**
- **Changes (spellings) for a verb in its past tense**
- **Changes (spellings) for the verb *be* in its present tense**
- **Changes (spellings) for the verb *be* in its past tense**

Teaching Helps

TEACHING SUGGESTION

Additional practice: An exercise that you might want to add here would be to have your students fill out the boxes in a grid that would have SINGULAR and PLURAL as types of "number" as column headings and FIRST, SECOND, and THIRD as types of "person" as row headings. First, they would put all of the personal pronouns in the right boxes. Later they would write out the spellings for a verb in its present and past tenses. Finally, they would write out the spellings for the verb *be* in its present and past tenses. They should write out the pronouns before the verbs (in parentheses, possibly, to differentiate them). See the "Final Test" section below.

ALTERNATIVE "EXAMPLES"

Again, here is alternative wording for some of the example material in the text. It can help you introduce the material in a way that is different from the book's.

PAGES	HEADING	EXAMPLES AS IN BOOK	ALTERNATIVE EXAMPLES
40	**Agreement of a Verb with Its Subject**	*Water evaporates.* *Buildings weaken.*	***Dust settles.*** ***Skies brighten.***

COMMENTS ON THE "REVIEW" SECTION [Text, 45]

Students MUST KNOW all the content of the review for this chapter—in their own words.

In addition, they should be able to fill out a chart that calls for correct number and person not only for ANY VERB—INCLUDING THE VERB *BE*—(in either the present or the past tense) but also for ALL THE PERSONAL PRONOUNS.

FINAL TEST

1. COMPLETE GRID A BY FILLING EVERY BOX WITH ONE PERSONAL PRONOUN THAT CORRECTLY FILLS IT.
2. COMPLETE GRID B BY FILLING THE BOXES (A) WITH THE PERSONAL PRONOUNS THAT CORRECTLY FILL THEM (SEE QUESTION 1) AND (B) ALL THE SPELLINGS OF THE **PRESENT TENSE OF THE VERB *JUMP*.** Each box will have two words—a pronoun and a verb word.
3. COMPLETE GRID C BY FILLING THE BOXES (A) WITH THE PERSONAL PRONOUNS THAT CORRECTLY FILL THEM (SEE QUESTION 1) AND (B) ALL THE SPELLINGS OF THE **PRESENT TENSE OF THE VERB *BE*.** Each box will have two words—a pronoun and a verb word.
4. COMPLETE GRID D BY FILLING THE BOXES (A) WITH THE PERSONAL PRONOUNS THAT CORRECTLY FILL THEM (SEE QUESTION 1) AND (B) WITH ALL THE SPELLINGS OF THE **PAST TENSE OF THE VERB *BE*.** Each box will have two words—a pronoun and a verb word.

Grid A

PERSON	NUMBER	
	Singular	Plural
First		
Second		
Third		

Grid B

PERSON	NUMBER	
	Singular	Plural
First		
Second		
Third		

Grid C

PERSON	NUMBER	
	Singular	Plural
First		
Second		
Third		

Grid D

PERSON	NUMBER	
	Singular	Plural
First		
Second		
Third		

Answers for the Final Test

Grid A

Person	Number	
	Singular	Plural
First	*I*	*we*
Second	*you*	*you*
Third	*he / she / it*	*they*

Grid B

Person	Number	
	Singular	Plural
First	*I jump*	*we jump*
Second	*you jump*	*you jump*
Third	*he jumps*	*they jump*

Grid C

Person	Number	
	Singular	Plural
First	*I am*	*we are*
Second	*you are*	*you are*
Third	*she is*	*they are*

Grid D

Person	Number	
	Singular	Plural
First	*I was*	*we were*
Second	*you were*	*you were*
Third	*it was*	*they were*

Possible Weighting of Answers for the Final Test

1. Each answer word is worth 4% (=32%).
2. Each verb word is worth 4% (=24%).
3. Each verb word is worth 4% (=24%).
4. Each verb word is worth 4% (=24%).

Chapter 4

More Information about Verbs

Objectives (Items in bolder letters are of greatest importance)

TO **LEARN TO REMEMBER** THESE TERMS/ITEMS:

- **Regular verb**
- **Irregular verb**
- **The spellings for all irregular verbs** (with practice)
- **Sentence** (with practice)
- **Command type of sentence** (with practice)
- **Present, past, and future tenses** (with practice)

TO BE ABLE TO WRITE: Commands; sentences in present, past, and future tenses

TO LEARN MORE ABOUT THESE TERMS/ITEMS:

- Dependent clause
- Words that introduce clauses
- The spellings for the verb *be* (with practice)
- The importance of verbs
- Misconceptions about ways to find verbs
- Introduction to successful strategies for finding verbs

Teaching Helps

CORRECTION (1991 Edition)

On page 56 of the text, the directives to DO Practices L and M belong ABOVE the paragraph directly above them that begins, "Grammarians...."

COMMENTS ON THE *SKILLS PRACTICE BOOK* AND *ANSWER BOOK*

Hung vs. hanged: *Hung* [Skills, 20, Practice C, number 21] is preferred to *hanged*, but *hanged* is acceptable when it means "hanged by the neck, especially if an act of execution."

TEACHING SUGGESTIONS

Practice with Irregular Verbs: The exercises on the irregular verbs (Practices A–F [Skills, 17–23] in this chapter) are tiresome to students because of their length and similarity. You can shorten them by having students fill out just the last two columns, the two most important ones. Also, you could assign these at intervals so that your students do two a night or so (possibly intermixed with some other types of exercise material).

Note, however, that I recommend that you give students even more practice with irregular verbs than the text offers BUT IN A DIFFERENT FORM—if for no other reason than that they are so important in the business world as a mark of someone "educated." One way to do this that might be fun for students is to pit groups of students against each other in contests to see which can do best. The object of the "game" would be to have them say (or write out) correctly all the spellings for the most important irregular verbs, especially the ones that they tend to misuse. For practice for the game, you can have them test each other (or test themselves at home) by using the "Basic" column to see whether they can fill in the blanks for the "Past Tense" and "After-had" columns especially. They might best do this by memorizing the four chief spellings of a verb AS A SET—for example, *go, going, went, gone; swim, swimming, swam, swum;* and so forth.

Note that RECOGNITION of irregular verbs in both their past tense and after-had spellings will be important in Chapters 6 and 7. To prepare your students for this, you could vary your game and/or their testing of each other or themselves by having them use the "Past Tense" and "After-had" columns (instead of the "Basic" column) to see whether they can NOW fill in the blanks for the "Basic" column (vs. the "Past Tense" and "After-had" columns). Note that for the "Past Tense" they would only use the verbs in Practices A and B [Skills, 17–18] (because for these verbs the "Past Tense" spellings differ from their "After-had " spellings), whereas for the "After-had" column they would use the verbs in all the Practices from A to F [Skills, 17–23]. Note that they would first have needed to fill these columns with the correct answers (let them complete the columns as assignments first; then have them write in the correct answers, possibly in a different color, so they can know which ones they need practice with). Possibly, you could combine my two suggestions so that they do the work of either two or three practices at a time and have games (and even quizzes) to test mastery of just these two or three sets at a time.

Note that a possible use of the "S/ES" and "ING" columns would be to give students practice in applying the chief spelling rules for adding suffixes to root words (see Text, 114); any such practice would simultaneously confirm in their minds that these are spellings that are characteristic of verbs.

Additional Practice (other than for irregular verbs): Because mastery instruction has not started yet, the goals of the text would not be served by adding extra practice (except for those that help students identify irregular verbs).

POINT TO BE NOTED

In the second example sentence at the top of page 54, the word *please* is doing the job of an adverb.

ALTERNATIVE "EXAMPLES"

Again, here is alternative wording for some of the example material in the text. It can help you introduce the material in a way that is different from the book's.

PAGES	HEADING	EXAMPLES AS IN BOOK	ALTERNATIVE EXAMPLES
46-47	**Spelling Patterns for Components of Main Verbs**	*halt* *wear*	***lift*** ***swear***
47	**Regular Verbs**	*plant / pull / listen*	***grow/teach/hurt***

PAGES	HEADING	EXAMPLES AS IN BOOK	ALTERNATIVE EXAMPLES
48-50	**Irregular Verbs**	*break* *lead* *cut* *see / freeze / sing* *tell / bring / say* *run / come / become* *hurt / rid / cost*	***swim*** ***stand*** ***quit*** ***know/steal/ring*** ***buy/pay/sling*** ***run/come/become*** ***let/bid/put***
51	**The Irregular Verb *Be***	*I am the goalie.* *You are a forward.* *She is a halfback.*	***I am content.*** ***You are content.*** ***He is content.***
54	**Importance of Verbs as Core of Sentences**	*Study with pen in hand.* *Please move to the right.* *Do not tell a lie.*	***Plan carefully.*** ***Please walk quietly.*** ***Do not be impolite.***
54-55	**Importance of Verbs as Core of Dependent Clauses**	*if it rains* *If it rains, the picnic will be postponed.*	***if the phone rings*** ***If the phone rings, it will be for me.***

COMMENTS ON THE "REVIEW" SECTION [Text, 60]

Students SHOULD KNOW all the content of the review for this chapter that is in darker lettering—in their own words.

Practically, they should know the difference between a regular and an irregular verb. In addition, they should be able to use all irregular verbs correctly (including the verb *be*), to write a sentence that expresses a command, and to write a sentence in either the present or past tense.

FINAL TEST

1. For each of these verbs, WRITE OUT BOTH ITS PAST TENSE AND AFTER-HAD SPELLINGS: *write, ride, bite, lie* (to rest), *bring, go, cut, pay, cling,* and *be*.
2. WRITE A SENTENCE THAT EXPRESSES A COMMAND.
3. WRITE A SENTENCE OF YOUR OWN THAT USES A VERB'S PAST TENSE COMPONENT TO FORM A PAST TENSE. Double underline that verb.
4. WRITE A SENTENCE OF YOUR OWN THAT USES A VERB'S BASIC COMPONENT TO FORM A PRESENT TENSE. Double underline that verb.

ANSWERS FOR THE FINAL TEST

1. *wrote, written; rode, ridden; bit, bitten; lay, lain; brought, brought; went, gone; cut, cut; paid, paid; clung, clung; was / were, been.*
2. *Watch the lightning.*
3. *Everyone laughed.*
4. *People plant flowers in spring.*

POSSIBLE WEIGHTING OF ANSWERS FOR THE FINAL TEST

1. Each answer is worth 4% (=80%).
2. The answer is worth 7% (=7%).
3. The answer is worth 7% (=7%).
4. The answer is worth 7% (=7%).

Chapter 5

Helping Verbs

Objectives (Items in bolder letters are of greatest importance)

TO **LEARN BY MEMORY:**

All the most common helping verbs

TO INTRODUCE ONLY THESE TERMS:

Contraction and "starter verb question"

Teaching Helps

TEACHING SUGGESTIONS

Teaching the Helping Verbs: Mastery of the helping verbs [Text, 61–76] is crucially important for success with this text. It is for this reason that I make two recommendations. One is that you insist on sheer memorization of the four groups of "starter" helping verbs and of the group of "follower" helping verbs. (To learn the nine starter helping verbs with no main-verb function, they might find it easiest to remember them in this order—*will, would; can, could; shall, should; may, might* and *must.*)

You can help their memorization by calling on students to say the groups of helpers for the class—and by doing this until most students know them cold. You can also help by giving repeated quizzes, even (after the first one or two) TIMED quizzes—maybe start by giving them a minute and a quarter to write down the twenty starters.

My second recommendation is that you always have them write these out as they take later tests and/or quizzes because they can then use their list as a checklist to be sure that they have not overlooked any in the sentences of the test or quiz. (In later tests, I would not count this as part of their test. It would just serve as a help for the test.)

The Role of the "Truths": The purpose of the "truths" sections of the text [Text, 56 ff.] is to supply background information in an interesting way. The purpose of the practice work that accompanies them is to lay a foundation for skills to be mastered at a later point or to deepen understanding and awareness of how English works.

Labeling Directives: Though the directives for labeling [Text, 68 ff.] are given as "required memory" throughout the text, they do not need to be strictly memorized because students learn them naturally as they apply them to the many sentences in the *Skills Practice Book.*

Truth C—the Need to Cover/Keep Hidden Duplicate Wording: You should make it clear to students at the point of the "Note" under the first example of Truth C [Text, 70] that THEY should NOT put lines through words in imitation of the text but that they SHOULD **PHYSICALLY** COVER any duplicate wording left behind as they shift words to do testing. This is an important principle for the remainder of this text. Show them (on an overhead projector if you can) just how they can do this. Use a finger or a pen or pencil to give them an example that they can imitate.

ALTERNATIVE "EXAMPLES"

Again, here is alternative wording for some of the example material in the text. It can help you introduce the material in a way that is different from the book's.

II-5: Helping Verbs

PAGES	HEADING	EXAMPLES AS IN BOOK	ALTERNATIVE EXAMPLES
62	Starters in the *Do* Set	*We do work hard. / We do the job.*	***We do try hard. / We do well.***
63	Starters in the *Have* Set	*We have won the game. / We have enough time.*	***We have returned. / We have a chance.***
65	Starters in the *Will* Set	*You will succeed.* *He would succeed if he tried.* *We can succeed next time.* *He could succeed if he tried.* *You shall not tell anyone.* *You should speak louder.* *You may not win.* *You might win.* *You must win.*	***I will remember.*** ***I would remember if I tried.*** ***I can remember sometimes.*** ***I could remember if I tried.*** ***You shall not forget it.*** ***You should use reminders.*** ***You may not forget.*** ***You might remember.*** ***You must remember.***
66–67	Truth A	*He can't say that we didn't help.*	***I don't see why we can't stay.***
68–69	Truth B	*He'd taken his time.* *He'd take his time.* *He's taking his time.* *He's sick.* *He's taken his time.*	***He'd broken a record.*** ***He'd break a record.*** ***He's breaking a record.*** ***He's a hero.*** ***He's broken a record.***
70	Truth C	*A team's coach can make a difference.* *Some of you didn't read the question carefully.*	***An honest day's work can pay off.*** ***Some of you didn't make any mistakes.***
71–72	Followers in the *Be* Set	*Jean will be coming. / Jean will be here.* *Jean is being told. / Jean is being a help.* *Jean has been invited. / Jean has been a boon.*	***Marge will be staying. / Marge will be early.*** ***Marge is being reminded. / Marge is being a comfort.*** ***Marge has been informed. / Marge has been a godsend.***
72–73	Follower in the *Have* Set	*They have left. / They will have left. / They have good news.*	***We have tried. / We will have tried. / We have the answers.***
73	Truth A	*This answer must not be correct.* *Stars can sometimes be brighter than usual.* *Computers have not always been around.*	***Deer must not be very smart.*** ***A dog can sometimes be unresponsive.*** ***Our mailman has not always been this early.***
74–75	Truth A	*Ed does sing well.* *Ed will sing well.* *The song is being sung.* *I was singing.* *It was sung.*	***June does dance well.*** ***June will dance well.*** ***The answer is being given.*** ***I was dancing.*** ***It was given.***

PAGES	HEADING	EXAMPLES AS IN BOOK	ALTERNATIVE EXAMPLES
74–75	**Truth A**	*The song has been sung.* *Ed may be singing.* *Ed has sung well.* *Ed could have sung well.*	***The answer has been given.*** ***June may be dancing.*** ***June has danced well.*** ***June could have danced well.***

COMMENTS ON THE "REVIEW" SECTION [Text, 76]

Students MUST KNOW the twenty starters and four followers both by memory and so they can identify them in writing.

Relative to starter verb questions, contractions, and labeling for inserted wording, they only need the experience provided in the practice material for now.

FINAL TEST

1. LIST ALL STARTER HELPING VERBS.
2. LIST ALL FOLLOWER HELPING VERBS.
3. PLACE A DOUBLE UNDERLINE UNDER ALL THE STARTER AND FOLLOWER HELPING VERBS IN THIS PASSAGE:

CAR SKATING

If you had been at our country place that day, you would have undergone an unusual experience. My family and I were all seated in the car as it was proceeding up our driveway. Though we had arranged that the heaviest children should sit in the back to put extra weight on the snow tires, our car could not be coaxed to skate uphill. Rather, its preference was clearly for sideways skating as an unsettling reverse of direction was occurring. Our car had no intentions of getting any of us onto the main road—which was the means by which we would have been visiting friends.

Fortunately, our friends could leave their house to pick us up. We did finally get to their place though we had had a scary moment. (It is hard for someone who has not experienced it to know what sliding backwards and sideways down over one hundred feet of driveway feels like.)

By the end of the day, our tractor was able to tow our station wagon back to the garage. This tractor has often been used in such emergencies. It has rarely let us down.

ANSWERS FOR THE FINAL TEST

1. *do, does, did; have, has, had; am, are, is, was, were; will, would, can, could, shall, should, may, might, must*
2. *be, being, been, have*
3. If you had been at our country place that day, you would have undergone an unusual experience. My family and I were all seated in the car as it was proceeding up our driveway. Though we had arranged that the heaviest children should sit in the back to put extra weight on the snow tires, our car could not be coaxed to skate uphill. Rather, its preference was clearly for sideways skating as an unsettling reverse of direction was occurring. Our car had no intentions of getting any of us onto the main road—which was the means by which we would have been visiting friends.

   Fortunately, our friends could leave their house to pick us up. We did finally get to their place though we had had a scary moment. (It is hard for someone who has not experienced it to know what sliding backwards and sideways down over one hundred feet of driveway feels like.)

   By the end of the day, our tractor was able to tow our station wagon back to the garage. This tractor has often been used in such emergencies. It has rarely let us down.

POSSIBLE WEIGHTING OF ANSWERS FOR THE FINAL TEST

1 Each answer (of 20) is worth 2% (=40%).
2. Each answer (of 4) is worth 2% (=8%).
3. Each answer (of 26) is worth 2% (=52%).

Chapter 6

Helping Verbs as Markers of Main Verbs

Objectives (Items in bolder letters are of greatest importance)

TO **LEARN BY MEMORY:**

How to find main verbs with total accuracy by means of the "Helpers plus WHAT/ING Word Verb Test"

TO INTRODUCE ONLY:

The role and importance of the "Tests (and Steps) to Follow to Succeed"

Teaching Helps

CORRECTION (1991 Edition)

Both of the charts that summarize the Helpers plus WHAT/ING Word Verb Test [Text, 95 and 98] have omitted Step 1 that follows the wording "Find the RIGHT *WHAT*-ANSWERING WORD." The Step 1 that was omitted states: **"Say the sentence through each starter or helper set AND ASK *WHAT*."** Note the revised wording for this subtest in the box to the right.

Not only those charts but also the chart on page 87 have omitted any mention of the need to label the main verbs. You could add this to the title of the ING Subtest in this way:

ING Subtest
(Label the Verbs)

> **Part B**
> **WHAT Subtest**
> **(To Find the Right *WHAT*-answering Word)**
>
> 1. **Say the sentence through each starter or helper set AND ASK *WHAT*.**
> 2. **REQUIREMENTS (to be the right *WHAT*-answering word):**
>   - **ONE word;**
>   - **MOST SENSE-COMPETING word;**
>   - **NEARBY word.**

TEACHING SUGGESTIONS

Truths about the Words That Make up Verb Phrases: These TRUTHS [Text, 77–79] lay a foundation for the rest of the chapter; they alert students to the importance of the TEST to come, the Helpers plus WHAT/ING Word Verb Test. You might show an example and then state the TRUTH. Subsequently, you or they could come up with another example or two. Then go on.

Labeling for Verbs [Text, 79]: Accept no other labeling than the double underline for a verb—the double underline causes the whereabouts of each verb word to be conspicuous (besides, the **single** underline is to be the label for verb words inside verb**al** phrases).

Introduction to the "Tests to Follow to Succeed" [Text, 80–81]: THE IMPORTANCE OF THESE TESTS AND THEIR ORDER—AND OF THE STEPS AND GROUND RULES INSIDE EACH TEST—CANNOT BE OVERSTATED. Because the

STEPS are taught one by one and cumulatively, your students will be able to verbalize them (and their order) by the end of the chapter. Have them do just that—that is, have them write out the STEPS of the TEST in their own words and in correct order. Then double check their wording for accuracy. Then permit this self-wording to be their "memorizing." They must never forget these STEPS or their ORDER. Review of them on a regular basis should become your standard way of proceeding.

I strongly recommend that you let the above suggestions be your guideline for all the TESTS in all the chapters to follow.

Memory Aid: This memory aid [Text, 80] will work for any/all the tests and may be an excellent way to have students learn them. For example, at the start of class once a week or so, you might have them test each other's knowledge of the order of the tests and of the steps and chief ground rules for each.

Overview for the Helpers plus WHAT/ING Word Verb Test [Text, 81]**:** This "Overview" section of a test serves to orient both you and the student to the goal of the test and the interrelationships of its parts. It supplies this information both in capsulized form and visually.

Part B: WHAT Subtest: The "Parts" of a Test will always be introduced in the same way as here [Text, 83–86]—first as a whole and second via a step-by-step set of explanations and practices. Again, the visual highlighting of just which part of the test is being treated is a help to both teacher and student.

You can always teach through examples **BUT** YOU MUST ALSO REQUIRE that students **VERBALIZE THE STEPS** SEVERAL TIMES.

Irregular Verb Exception [Text, 91–92]**:** It is for this exception that recognition of irregular verbs in their after-had spelling is of special importance.

POINT TO BE NOTED

There is a phenomenon in English that you may want to note. Sometimes one main verb uses TWO WORDS to carry a SINGLE MEANING. Here is an example:

Our cake TURNED OUT a success.

[Notice that you can substitute *did turn* for *turned* but that the word *out* has no intrinsic feature to help you identify it.]

The proof that the two words *turned out* are a "two-word" verb is that you can replace them with a single word, the word *proved,* that has comparable meaning. You can substitute the sentence *Our cake PROVED a success* for the sentence *Our cake TURNED OUT a success.*

Note that students would be expected to label only the first of two such words a verb if an idiom like this should appear in a practice sentence. (They would only know that the second word is an extension of the verb if you were to tell them, but I do not necessarily recommend that at this introductory level.)

ALTERNATIVE "EXAMPLES"

Again, here is alternative wording for some of the example material in the text. It can help you introduce the material in a way that is different from the book's.

PAGES	HEADING	EXAMPLES AS IN BOOK	ALTERNATIVE EXAMPLES
78	**Truth C**	*Even deep snow will eventually melt.* *History is being too quickly forgotten.*	***Skillfully arranged twigs will always burn.*** ***Fallen toys can be too easily disregarded.***

II-6: Helping Verbs as Markers of Main Verbs

PAGES	HEADING	EXAMPLES AS IN BOOK	ALTERNATIVE EXAMPLES
78	Truth D	*Everyone is out during the lunch hour.* *Roses have a delicate fragrance.*	***The toddler's toys were everywhere.*** ***The plan had no backers.***
79	Truth E	*Marge will be the captain.* *People in the suburbs must have their own cars.*	***The summer will be over soon.*** ***The box will have several holes.***
82	Helper Set	*could have come* *could have been included* *might then have lost* *should not ever have been forgotten*	***will be singing*** ***will have been invited*** ***could eventually have won*** ***should not ever have been discarded***
84	Asking *WHAT* Right the First Time	*Each person will have received a turn.* *Carlos has a brand new shirt.* *Pam could as easily change her plans.*	***The books will be returned on time.*** ***The pitcher had some tricky pitches.*** ***Bruce could as easily bunt this time.***
85	Asking *WHAT* Right Again	*As the jogger was running, he was almost blinded by the rays of the sun but was being cheered by the singing of the birds.*	***Since the hurricane was approaching, people had been told to evacuate so they were first preparing their belongings.***
85-86	Asking *WHAT* in Sentences with *Not*	*The storm has not appeared yet.* *Some wildflowers do not bloom for long.*	***The windows had not been opened yet.*** ***The door would not shut tight.***
88-89	Part C, 1: Adding *Ing*	*He has come early.* *He has dimes in his pocket.* *They will soon succeed.* *Everyone was late.* *The wind is steadier.* *We were the helpers.*	***No one could feel the difference.*** ***People have principles that guide their lives.*** ***We could not easily hurry.*** ***No one was unprepared.*** ***The sun is brighter.*** ***They were visitors.***
89-90	Part C, 2: The *Ed* Exception	*A few have walked that far.* *This bench is rugged.*	***Everything has worked so far.*** ***The picture is crooked.***

PAGES	HEADING	EXAMPLES AS IN BOOK	ALTERNATIVE EXAMPLES
90-91	**Part C, 2: The *Ing* Exception**	*Jack is fixing his car.* *Time is unceasing.*	***The dog is wagging his tail.*** ***Drunkenness is unfulfilling.***
91-92	**Part C, 2: Irregular Verb Exception**	*I have swum there.* *We are taught English.*	***This plant has grown inside.*** ***A few crabs were caught today.***
93-94	**Part C, 3: Testing for Sameness of Meaning**	*The box is empty.* *Paco had trouble with his car yesterday.* *Mary is willing to help.*	***That dress is pretty.*** ***We had fish for dinner.*** ***The years of worry have been telling.***
96	**Endnotes: Verb Phrases**	*Fred may have been only kidding.* *Expensive items can sometimes be easily broken.*	***The stars have only been hiding.*** ***Autumn days can sometimes be unhappily experienced in August.***
96	**Endnotes: Wording after Helpers**	*The appointment will be soon.* *My book is home.*	***Our next game will be Friday.*** ***Wildflowers are everywhere.***
96	**Endnotes: Phrases and Noun Clauses**	*Tardiness is to arrive late for something.* *The fact is that college graduates can earn impressive salaries.*	***Happiness is to pursue a noble purpose.*** ***The reason for winning was that we had trained well.***

COMMENTS ON THE "ENDNOTES" SECTION [Text, 96–97]

The endnotes in this chapter should be included in your teaching. The first two have immediate application and will help your students either prevent mistakes or correct them once they have been made. The last one lays the foundation for later instruction.

COMMENTS ON THE "REVIEW" SECTION [Text, 97-98]

The Helpers plus WHAT/ING Word Verb Test [Text, 98] needs the added wording: **Say the sentence through each starter or helper set AND ASK *WHAT*.** Note the section above entitled "Correction (1991 Edition)."

Note that this test must be known by students like the palm of their hands—not in exactly these words but both operationally and in written-out wording that is correct relative to MEANING and ORDER.

FINAL TEST

1. Write out all the STARTER HELPING VERBS.
2. Write out all the FOLLOWER HELPING VERBS.
3. Write out all the STEPS AND REQUIREMENTS OF THE WHAT SUBTEST of the Helpers plus WHAT/ING Word Verb Test.

4. Write out all the STEPS AND REQUIREMENTS OF THE ING SUBTEST of the Helpers plus WHAT/ING Word Verb Test.
5. Apply the Helpers plus WHAT/ING Word Verb Test throughout the passage below. DOUBLE UNDERLINE ALL VERB WORDS.

NOTE-TAKING

At least at the college level, students must take notes during lecture time if they do not wish to be at a serious disadvantage. Students who have chosen not to take notes have thereby discarded their chance of having a written account of what was taught. They have consequently doomed themselves to virtual guesswork on quizzes and tests.

Such students must be unaware that teachers are known to base their tests mostly on what they have explained in class. They expect students to know all that has ever been said in class. In their minds, this is what they were hired for—to be interpreters of the subject matter so that students will gain their wisdom regarding the subject that they are learning.

ANSWERS FOR THE FINAL TEST

1. *will, would; can, could; shall, should; may, might, must; do, does, did; have, has, had; are, am, is, was, were*
2. *be, being, been, have*
3. (a) Say all/enough of the words of the sentence through each starter or helper set; (b) ask *what*; (c) the answer must be ONE word; (d) the answer must be the MOST SENSE-COMPLETING word; (e) the answer must be NEARBY.
4. (a) Add *ing* to the word; (b) AS IT STANDS (c) OUTSIDE THE SENTENCE; (d) exception: replace *ed* with *ing*; (e) exception: drop *ing*; (f) exception: IRREGULAR VERBS ARE VERBS—you must recognize them; (g) test for sameness of dictionary meaning.
5. At least at the college level, students must take notes during lecture time if they do [don't] not wish to be at a serious disadvantage. Students who have chosen not to take notes have thereby discarded their chance of having a written account of what was taught. They have consequently doomed themselves to virtual guesswork on quizzes and tests.

   Such students must be unaware (✓) that teachers are known to base their tests mostly on what they have explained in class. They expect students to know all that has ever been said in class. In their minds, this is what (✓) they were hired for—to be interpreters of the subject matter so that students will gain their wisdom regarding the subject that they are learning.

[The placing of check marks and adding of *[don't]* could be given bonus credit. Note that what answers *WHAT* after *is* (at the start of the last sentence) is really the rest of the sentence. Since you could not expect students to determine this on their own so early in the text, you could give them credit for placing a check mark under the word *what* (which is the best that you can expect of them at this point).]

POSSIBLE WEIGHTING OF ANSWERS FOR THE FINAL TEST

1. Each word is worth ½ point (=10%)
2. Each word is worth ½ point (=2%)
3. Each "part" is worth 4 points (=20%)
4. Each "part" is worth 4 points (=28%)
5. Each of the 28 words is worth 1½ points (42%)—any error would mean the loss of 1½ points

Chapter 7

Remaining Main Verbs

Objectives (Items in bolder letters are of greatest importance)

TO **LEARN BY MEMORY:**

How to find verbs by means of the "Do/Does/Did Test (to Find Remaining Verbs)"—with total accuracy

TO INTRODUCE ONLY:

The importance of the GROUND RULES for the "Tests (and Steps) to Follow to Succeed"

Teaching Helps

TEACHING SUGGESTIONS

Truths about Remaining Main Verbs: These truths [Text, 99–104] supply the background that will help students learn the TEST in this chapter both more easily and more lastingly.

Truth E [Text, 103]**:** This do/does/did substitution is a powerful strategy because it enables you to tell whether a word that looks like a verb (such as *crossed* in the example) is in fact functioning as a verb with complete accuracy.

New Terms: These new terms [Text, 101–102] have importance inside this chapter alone; they help simplify the instruction here.

Ground Rules for the Tests to Follow to Succeed [Text, 105]**:** Notice that the GROUND RULES for a test have the same importance as the test's STEPS have. However, there are two differences. One is that the order of execution of the ground rules rarely has importance; the other is that the ground rules rarely have to be committed to memory—they become "owned" through the amount of practice supplied.

Labeling for Inserted Wording [*See* Text, 68]**:** Though the 1991 edition of the text does not say so explicitly in this chapter, there is a required labeling for the *do*/*does*/*did* substitutions—namely: the TWO words must be written out and enclosed in SIDE BRACKETS ([ ]), and the place of insertion (before the verb) must be marked by a caret (^). Students have been doing this in Chapter 5 [Text, 68–69] and since Chapter 6 [Text, 85 ff.]; this labeling will be a requirement throughout the text.

Spelling Tips: The three spelling rules identified here [Text, 114] are the ones that have the fewest exceptions and that apply to an extremely large number of words.

Step 3 [Text, 119–20]**:** It is because of this step that recognition of irregular verbs in their past-tense spellings is of special importance.

ALTERNATIVE "EXAMPLES"

Again, here is alternative wording for some of the example material in the text. It can help you introduce the material in a way that is different from the book's.

PAGES	HEADING	EXAMPLES AS IN BOOK	ALTERNATIVE EXAMPLES
99-100	**Truth A**	*That orange tasted good.* *This orange tastes good.* *Oranges taste good.* *We ate the oranges.*	***The blue jay stayed the winter.*** ***The blue jay stays the winter.*** ***Blue jays stay the winter.*** ***The blue jays made a lot of noise.***
101	**Truth C**	*Joe did need a break.* *Joe does need a break.* *We do need a break.* *They did take a break.*	***Sue did need a dollar.*** ***Sue does need a dollar.*** ***We do need a dollar.*** ***We did bring a dollar.***
102-103	**Truth D**	*A fox crossed the road.* *The borrowed rope that Ed used lacked the needed strength.*	***We braved the storm.*** ***The discolored ball that the children selected needed more air.***
103	**Truth E**	*The crossed wires caused a spark.*	***The opened door caused a draft.***
104	**Truth F**	*Speak distinctly.* *I know the person you mean.* *The book Paul borrowed belongs to the library.*	***Stand up straight.*** ***I bring the things I need.*** ***The clock Meg uses runs on batteries.***
104	**Truth G**	*The twig that the bird carried fell to the ground when a sound surprised and frightened it.*	***The pen I bought writes poorly because it drags and makes unwanted marks.***
107	**Ground Rule 1**	*He has arrived already.*	***He has left a note.***
108	**Ground Rule 3**	*Deer eat the branches of young fruit trees.*	***Clipboards keep sheets of paper from getting lost.***
108	**Ground Rule 4**	*I do care.* *He does care.* *We did care.*	***I do swim.*** ***He does swim.*** ***We did swim.***
109	**Ground Rule 5**	*A toasted sandwich has special appeal.* *The people who objected were misinformed.*	***A burned pan needs special attention.*** ***The woman who helped was a stranger.***

PAGES	HEADING	EXAMPLES AS IN BOOK	ALTERNATIVE EXAMPLES
110	**Ground Rule 6**	*He used some borrowed equipment.*	***The car used some imported components.***
110-111	**Ground Rule 7**	*The answer John gave proved wrong.*	***The car we rented handled well.***
113	***Ed* Words That Cannot Be Verbs**	*rugged* *unwanted*	***ragged*** ***unintended***
114	**Spelling Rule: Y to I**	*deny* *empty*	***imply*** ***hurry***
115	**Spelling Tip A**	*carried* *replied*	***readied*** ***allied***
116	**Step 2: Explanation**	*Careful reading takes longer.* *A mistake deserves analysis.*	***A canoe seems unsafe.*** ***A canoe travels faster.***
117	***S/es* Words That are not Detachable**	*glass / fuss / sometimes / his*	***loss / dress / always / this***
117	***S/es* Words That Cannot be Verbs**	*ideas / yes / cars / moss*	***classes / its / bells / less***
117	**Spelling Rule for *Y* to *IE*** [See box.]	*deny* *fancy*	***fry*** ***bully***
118	**Spelling Tip D**	*carries* *replies*	***studies*** ***dries***
120-121	**Step 4**	*We need more money.*	***We spend carefully.***
121	**Explanation**	*arrival / standing / talker / weak*	***survival / leaning / driver / stale***
123	**Endnote**	*Children often play hopscotch.*	***Wind storms rarely last long.***

Comment on the "Endnotes" Section [Text, 96–97]

This endnote [Text, 123] could be omitted if there is a shortage of time.

Comments on the "Review" Section [Text, 123–24]

The order of the tests must be known.

The meanings of the *do/does/did* substitutions should not need further emphasis.

The spelling tips are important operationally but do not need to be remembered as such. The Do/does/did Test itself is the second foundation for this text (after the Helpers plus

WHAT/ING Word Verb Test); students must be able to tell you this whole test in their own words and accurately.

FINAL TEST

1. Explain WHICH WORDS YOU MUST TEST with the Do/does/did Test.
2. Tell the ONLY SPELLING OF A VERB that you may use after *do, does,* or *did.* Give an example.
3. Write out clearly the ONLY TRUE PROOF that the Do/does/did Test has identified a verb word.
4. What are the TWO CONDITIONS with which you MUST TEST with *did?*
5. When MUST YOU TEST with *does?*
6. When MUST YOU TEST with *do?*
7. Apply both the Helpers plus WHAT/ING Word Verb Test and the Do/does/did Test throughout the passage below. DOUBLE UNDERLINE ALL VERB WORDS. (Be sure to write out—and correctly—all required do/does/did substitutions.)

UNFIT FENCING

There is such a thing as deterioration. What deteriorates fastest around a horse farm seems to be the fencing that the horseman owns. At least, this has now happened to me.

While my wife and I were savoring our second cup of coffee this morning, our phone rang. A neighbor was calling; he wanted to report an untethered horse that he could see munching on the grass before his eyes as he spoke. He wondered whether it could possibly be mine. Knowing that my neighbor had more than likely called just the right person, I did not dodge the truth but admitted the possibility that the horse might indeed be mine. I promised that an investigation would be immediately initiated.

First, I got dressed in appropriate clothing. Then I rounded up some kind of rope. Finally, I went to my neighbor's and took possession of the horse that indeed was mine.

What had happened might have been predicted. Both strands of the barbed wiring that had enclosed my corral on the neighbor's side had snapped during the summer. Since I had put the horse in her enclosure during a snowstorm, I had been unable to check the fencing. The lesson learned may be to check my fencing on a periodic basis.

ANSWERS FOR THE FINAL TEST

1. All the words that have not been already labeled as verbs (all NON-double underlined words).
2. The basic spelling—*does swim.*
3. The substitute spelling must cause the whole sentence to make sense as English.
4. (a) When the word ends in *ed;* (b) when the word is an irregular verb in a past tense form.
5. When the word ends in detachable *s/es.*
6. Whenever the conditions in the answers to questions 4 and 5 do not prevail (for all OTHER words—except the first of the sentence).
7. There is such a thing as deterioration. What [does deteriorate] deteriorates fastest around a horse farm [does seem] seems to be the fencing that the

[does own]
horseman ^owns. At least, this has now happened to me.

[did ring]
While my wife and I were savoring our second cup of coffee this morning, our phone ^rang. A neighbor was calling; he

[did want] [did speak] [did wonder]
^wanted to report an untethered horse that he could see munching on the grass before his eyes as he ^spoke. He ^wondered whether it could possibly be mine. Knowing that my neighbor had more than likely called just the right person, I did not

[did admit] [did promise]
dodge the truth but ^admitted the possibility that the horse might indeed be mine. I ^promised that an investigation would be immediately initiated.

[did get] [did round] [did go]
First, I ^got dressed in appropriate clothing. Then I ^rounded up some kind of rope. Finally, I ^went to my neighbor's

[did take]
and ^took possession of the horse that indeed was mi✓ne.

What had happened might have been predicted. Both strands of the barbed wiring that had enclosed my corral on the neighbor's side had snapped during the summer. Since I had put the horse in her enclosure during a snowstorm, I had been una✓ble to check the fencing. The lesson learned may be to check my fencing on a periodic basis.

[Students must write out all the do/does/did substitutions. In addition, these are weighted as TWO ANSWERS in this test **and** in all subsequent (final) tests. Again, the check marks could be given bonus credit; they have not been considered required answers here.]

Possible Weighting of Answers for the Final Test

1. This answer is worth 10%.
2. This answer is worth 5%.
3. This answer is worth 5%.
4. Each answer is worth 5% (=10%).
5. This answer is worth 5%.
6. This answer is worth 5%.
7. Each of the 63 answers is worth 1% (=63%).

Chapter 8

Simpler Questions

Objectives (Items in bolder letters are of greatest importance)

TO **LEARN BY MEMORY** these terms/items:
- **Movable Starter**
- **Main subject**
- **A revised order for carrying out the tests**
- **The STEPS for the Main Subject Test—for Questions** (the ground rules become learned through repeated application)

TO INTRODUCE ONLY THESE TERMS:
- Core verb
- Sentence unit

Teaching Helps

COMMENT ON THE ORDER OF THE CHAPTERS

It is easier for students to shift the starter that changes questions to statements (and statements to questions)—the MOVABLE STARTER—in questions than in statements. It is for this reason alone that this chapter precedes Chapters 9 and 10. This chapter introduces the strategy of shifting the verb to identify the key elements of the sentence in such a way as to build self-confidence and to establish the meanings of the key terms MOVABLE STARTER and MAIN SUBJECT.

TEACHING SUGGESTION

Truths about the Chief Parts of a Sentence: As usual, these truths [Text, 125–27] lay the foundation for the definitions and the TEST that follow. In addition, they lay the foundation for the work of both of the two chapters that follow this one. Therefore, give these truths adequate emphasis in your teaching.

CLARIFICATIONS

Core Verbs: A CORE VERB [Text, 131] is a verb whose starter is a movable starter; it is ALSO a verb that expresses a command (this will be added to the next edition in parentheses).

Sentence Unit: A SENTENCE UNIT [Text, 132] includes both the main clause and all the grammatical units that modify it—even when these are dependent clauses; school grammars try to differentiate "main clauses" from the "dependent clauses" that complete their meaning.

ALTERNATIVE "EXAMPLES"

Again, here is alternative wording for some of the example material in the text. It can help you introduce the material in a way that is different from the book's.

PAGES	HEADING	EXAMPLES AS IN BOOK	ALTERNATIVE EXAMPLES
126-127	Truth A	*My book was in the kitchen.* *My book can be in the kitchen.* *My book stays in the kitchen.*	***My hammer was in its place.*** ***My hammer could be in its place.*** ***My hammer stays in its place.***
126	Truth B	*The wall clock has lost time.*	***The answer has escaped him.***
126-127	Truth C	*Can't advertising be misleading?*	***Couldn't guessing be hazardous?***
127	Truth D	*Air that is damp can cause discomfort.*	***A draft that is excessive can be harmful.***
128-129	Label: Movable Starters	*A cloud can shield one's eyes from the sun.* *Does acid rain harm plants?* *Rain without wind seems less threatening.*	***A mug can hold more fluid than a cup.*** ***Does a dull scissors cut poorly?*** ***The height of flowers varies.***
130	Label: Main Subjects	*Many hours have gone by.*	***Little discussion has taken place.***
134	Ground Rule 1	*Do sensible students check their own work?*	***Do successful students ask questions?***
135	Ground Rule 2	*Aren't birds considered animals?* *Is all drinking water free of minerals?* *Can't children also help with the dishes?*	***Aren't bats considered pests?*** ***Is water from a stream fit for drinking?*** ***Can't children also have valuable insights?***
136	Ground Rule 3	*Should someone who uses a saw wear goggles?* *Can a girl who is getting good grades overwork?*	***Should a child who plays with fire be punished?*** ***Can a boy who is neglecting his homework be neglecting his future?***
138	Step 2	*Do few birds stay in the same location all summer?*	***Do dirty car windows give reason for concern?***
141	Endnotes: Counterpart Subjects	*Doesn't anybody agree?* *Somebody doesn't agree.*	***Isn't anybody listening?*** ***Somebody isn't listening.***

PAGES	HEADING	EXAMPLES AS IN BOOK	ALTERNATIVE EXAMPLES
141	**Endnotes: Job of Non-movable Starters**	*We were enjoying the movie though we had already seen it.*	***We were resting because the day had gotten so hot.***

COMMENTS ON THE "ENDNOTES" SECTION [Text, 96–97]

Counterpart Subjects: This endnote [Text, 141] could be omitted if there is a shortage of time.

Job of Nonmovable Starters: You should include this endnote [Text, 141–42] in your teaching because it lays the foundation for later instruction.

COMMENTS ON THE "REVIEW" SECTION [Text, 60]

The NEW order of the tests must be known.

The STEPS for the Main Subject Test—for Questions, like the steps for all the TESTS, must be known well enough that students can tell you ALL THE STEPS **and** IN THE RIGHT ORDER in their own words and accurately. Note that the repetition built into the exercises of the text should be sufficient for the remembering of the ground rules (for this test).

Note that the terms **sentence unit** and **core verb** come to be learned EXPERIENTIALLY as a fruit of doing the exercises of the text.

FINAL TEST

1. According to your text, WHERE DO YOU FIND A MAIN SUBJECT?
2. [For bonus credit] (What else does the text say is true about the words that make up the main subject?)
3. What is meant by the term MOVABLE STARTER?
4. In starter verb questions, WHERE DO YOU FIND THE MOVABLE STARTER?
5. In starter verb questions, WHERE DO YOU SHIFT THE MOVABLE STARTER TO?
6. In starter verb questions, WHERE DO YOU FIND THE COMPANION VERBS (if any) for a movable starter?
7. LIST ALL THE TESTS—IN CORRECT ORDER.
8. Apply BOTH verb tests **and** the Main Subject Test—for Questions to the passage below. Make sure that you write out correctly all required do/does/did substitutions and that you DOUBLE UNDERLINE ALL VERB WORDS and LABEL NEATLY ALL SUBJECT WORDING.

EXERCISING

Can a person who likes to get exercise jog during all the seasons of the year? This depends on the person or persons. Would such people mind running when the temperature is near zero? Would they hesitate to jog when they must run on ice-covered roads? Wouldn't they be foolhardy to jog if snow was falling heavily? Shouldn't these people think twice about running when the temperature is over 90? You may even know someone who jogs even when the conditions are uninviting. Wouldn't a person who lives in a country place be one who might most easily jog in all seasons?

ANSWERS FOR THE FINAL TEST

1. Between the two positions of a movable starter.
2. (They must belong together, and they must be doing the job of subject. [You could count EITHER answer as a right answer.])
3. The starter verb that can be repositioned to create or undo a question. [any comparable wording]
4. At the start of the sentence.
5. To where it fits inside a sentence.
6. After the movable starter in its inside (shifted-to) position.
7. Main Subject Test—for Questions, Helpers plus WHAT/ING Word Verb Test, Do/does/did Test.

8. MS Can Ⓢ a person who [does like] likes to get exercise [can] jog during all the seasons of the year? This [does depend] depends on the persons or persons. MS Would Ⓢ such people [would] mind running when the temperature is near zero? MS Would Ⓢ they [would] hesitate to jog when they must run on ice-covered roads? MS Wouldn't Ⓢ they [would] be foolhardy ✓ to jog if snow was falling heavily? MS Shouldn't Ⓢ these people [should] think twice about running when the temperature is over 90? You may even know someone who [does jog] jogs even when the conditions are uninviting ✓. MS Wouldn't Ⓢ a person who [does live] lives in a country place [would] be ✓ one who might most easily jog in all seasons?

POSSIBLE WEIGHTING OF ANSWERS FOR THE FINAL TEST

1–6. Each answer is worth 6% (=30/36%).

7. 6% (3% for inclusion of all tests; 3% for listing them in the right order).

8. 64½%. Each verb word is worth 1½% (31 x 1½ = 46½%); each movable starter is worth 1½% (6 x 1½ = 9%); each main subject is worth 1½% (6 x 1½ = 9%). [The check marks have not been considered required answers.]

Chapter 9

The Helper That Shifts—in Statements

Objectives (Items in bolder letters are of greatest importance)

TO LEARN BY MEMORY: **The order for carrying out the tests**

TO LEARN BY EXPERIENCE: The steps and ground rules for the Movable Starter Test

Teaching Helps

CORRECTION (1991 Edition)

The directive to do Practice E (near the top of page 156) is misplaced. It belongs at the very bottom of the same page—at the end of the commentary on Ground Rule 3.

COMMENT ON THE SUBJECT MATTER OF THE CHAPTER

This TEST is so natural that virtually all students carry out all its ground rules flawlessly and subconsciously when they create their own questions. However, these GROUND RULES need to be LEARNED before students can handle the sentences **that others have created**.

Though the ground rules might seem like a burden for your students to remember, they will find themselves remembering them naturally due to the amount of practice supplied and because they learn them ONE AT A TIME and CUMULATIVELY.

COMMENTS ON TWO OF THE TRUTHS

Truths about the Ways to Find Main Subjects: These truths are designed to establish the helpfulness and importance of the strategy of this chapter as the strategy of choice for finding main subjects.

Truths about the Chief Parts of Sentences: These truths serve as an introduction to the Movable Starter Test and should be helpful (and reassuring) to students.

POINT TO BE NOTED

There is a problem with carrying out the Movable Starter Test with the sentence *Those who learn best review regularly.* For this sentence (and others like it that have two verbs and both are in the present tense without an *s*/*es* spelling), the Movable Starter Test has a special requirement. This is that you WHEN YOU TEST FOR THE MOVABLE STARTER, YOU KEEP THE DO SUBSTITUTE SPELLINGS FOR BOTH VERBS ACTIVE **AT THE SAME TIME**.

For example, for testing purposes, the

sentence becomes AND STAYS *Those who do learn best do review regularly.* When you test this sentence, it will sound WRONG to say *Do those who learn best do review regularly.* On the other hand, it will sound RIGHT to say *Do those who do learn best review regularly.* I have tried to eliminate all such sentences from the practice material.

ALTERNATIVE "EXAMPLES"

Again, here is alternative wording for some of the example material in the text. It can help you introduce the material in a way that is different from the book's.

PAGES	HEADING	EXAMPLES AS IN BOOK	ALTERNATIVE EXAMPLES
145	**Truth B**	*My sister saw smoke outside her window that looked as if it was coming from a fire.*	***My brother heard a news report that an earthquake had struck a city in Asia.***
146	**Truth C**	*The bike I am now riding lacks the brakes I need for steep hills.*	***The typewriter that my parents once used lacked any ability to store what had been typed.***
147	**Truth D**	*The midsummer variety of birds differs from the spring variety.*	***The bright red colors of a summer bush can be the first sign of fall.***
147-148	**Truth A**	*The thunderstorm that brought much-needed coolness caused unneeded flooding.*	***The proof that it rained heavily lies in the puddles of water on the ground.***
151	**Step 1**	*The tomatoes in the bag had fallen through.*	***The jar on the shelf had fallen.***
152	**Step 2**	*The place where Dad had put the old toy that we were looking for was the garbage can.*	***The scissors that we have been keeping in a kitchen drawer where we can find them have disappeared.***
155	**Ground Rule 2**	*The delay was not longer than expected.*	***The ink was not blue.***
156	**Ground Rule 3**	*The bat that Pete thinks he broke needs some tape.*	***The watch that Bill thinks he lost appears to be found.***
157	**Ground Rule 4**	*Andrew does his work rapidly.* *Maria had band in the sixth period today.*	***Pablo does subtractions in his head.*** ***Michelle had pancakes for breakfast.***

PAGES	HEADING	EXAMPLES AS IN BOOK	ALTERNATIVE EXAMPLES
158	**Sentences Contrasting the Uses of Do/does/did**	*Tom does work hard. / Tom does well.* *I do play the piano. / I do my best.* *They did leave early. / They did a lot.*	***Jack does like to work. / Jack does the dishes.*** ***We do plan everything. / We do the essential things first.*** ***They did come early. / They did their share.***
158	**Sentences Contrasting the Uses of Have/has/had**	*Tom has left. / Tom has plans.* *I have won. / I have some.* *They had forgotten. / They had fewer players.*	***Pam has stayed. / Pam has style.*** ***We have succeeded. / We have a few.*** ***They had come. / They had left-overs.***
162	**Ground Rule 6**	*The package that came yesterday had been damaged.*	***The rain that fell yesterday was absorbed into the ground.***
163	**Ground Rule 7**	*The apples will be plentiful this year.*	***The blueberries will be late this year.***
163	**Ground Rule 8**	*A bird that stays north in the winter is the chickadee.*	***A mist that settles everywhere will soon disappear.***

COMMENT ON THE "REVIEW" SECTION [Text, 165-66]

These STEPS and the GROUND RULES should become so learned through the amount of practice provided here that students will not need to commit them to memory.

FINAL TEST

1. LIST ALL THE TESTS—IN CORRECT ORDER.
2. Tell the REASON WHY YOU MUST **PHYSICALLY** COVER ITEMS AS YOU CARRY OUT THE MOVABLE STARTER TEST.
3. Give THREE EXAMPLES OF TYPES OF WORDING THAT YOU MUST PHYSICALLY COVER as you carry out this test.
4. For the passage below, CARRY OUT ALL OF THE TESTS TO FOLLOW TO SUCCEED THAT YOU NOW KNOW—IN THE RIGHT ORDER. Make sure that you write out correctly all the do/does/did substitutions as you double underline verbs and that you label required main subject wording. (Bonus credit is available if you label ALL main subjects.)

SELF-DEPENDENCE

A girl that I know has rarely asked her parents for money. Isn't this an extraordinary quality? She would baby-sit whenever a chance presented itself. This girl, who also was getting nearly the best grades in her class, worked after school during her senior year. Wasn't her wish that her father would not be burdened by debt on her account when she went to college?

A girl who has this much determination will achieve great things. Wouldn't you agree that she deserved to win a full-tuition scholarship to the college that she had chosen?

Answers for the Final Test

1. Main Subject Test—for Questions, Helpers plus WHAT/ING Word Verb Test, Do/does/did Test, Movable Starter Test.
2. You may not say/use any word twice in the same sentence.
3. Starter/starter + *n't*, starter + *not*, core verb (because of its do/does/did substitution), a do/does/did substitution that is not now being tested.
4.

Ⓢ
[has] [do know] MS
A girl that I know has rarely asked her parents for money.

MS Ⓢ [is]
Isn't this an extraordinary quality?

[would] Ⓢ
She ✓

MS [did present]
would baby-sit whenever a chance presented itself.

[did] Ⓢ
This girl, who also was getting nearly the best grades in her class,

MS
[did work]
worked after school during her senior year.

MS Ⓢ [was]
Wasn't her wish that her father would not be burdened by debt on her account when she

[did go]
went to college?

Ⓢ
[will] [does have] MS
A girl who has this much determination will achieve great things.

MS Ⓢ [would]
Wouldn't you agree that she

[did deserve]
deserved to win a full-tuition scholarship to the college that she had chosen?

Possible Weighting of Answers for the Final Test

1. 9% (3 for inclusion of all tests; 3 for listing them in correct order).
2. 5%.
3. Each answer is worth 4% (12%).
4. Each answer of the 39 answers is worth 1.9% (each verb word is one answer and, in addition, each correctly labeled movable starter is one more answer) 74%. (The four bonus answers can be worth any amount you wish.)

Chapter 10

Finding Main Subjects in Statements

Objectives (Items in bolder letters are of greatest importance)

TO LEARN BY MEMORY:
Main Subject Test—for Statements
Order in which to carry out the tests

TO LEARN BY EXPERIENCE how to tell the main subject from nearby wording

TO APPRECIATE the role of sentences with space-filler *there* occupying the subject territory

Teaching Helps

TEACHING SUGGESTIONS

Orientation. Though your students have already learned how to find the main subject in statements, they have yet to learn to differentiate between the subject wording and adverbial wording that also can stand between the two positions of a movable starter. They also must learn how space-filler *there* can fill the subject territory in a unique way.

Writing Tips for Using Space-filler *There*: This section [Text, 174-75] would be a perfect occasion to ask students to write paragraphs that have a space-filler *there* sentence as their topic sentence. You could supply them with possible topics, such as Rules for Bike Riders, Rules for Being a Good Friend, Steps for Baking a Cake, and so forth.

ALTERNATIVE "EXAMPLES"

Again, here is alternative wording for some of the example material in the text. It can help you introduce the material in a way that is different from the book's.

PAGES	HEADING	EXAMPLES AS IN BOOK	ALTERNATIVE EXAMPLES
169	Step 1	*The first frost of the fall kills flowers that have not been covered.*	***The roar of a brook reminds a listener that much rain has fallen.***
169-70	Wording Not Belonging with the Subject	*We seldom discussed the matter.*	***We usually jog in the evening.***
170-71	Step 2	*There is a new plan.* *There are two new plans.*	***There is a new book.*** ***There are two new books.***

PAGES	HEADING	EXAMPLES AS IN BOOK	ALTERNATIVE EXAMPLES
170-71	**Step 2**	*There is nothing to fear.* *There was an explosion.* *There are answers here.*	***There is another rake.*** ***There was a parade.*** ***There is a plant here.***
173	**Wording Not Belonging with a Subject in Such Sentences**	*There was a tornado here last year.*	***There was a broken fire extinguisher here last year.***
174-75	**Writing Tips for Using Space-filler *There***	*There are several reasons why a person should exercise.* *"First, there are those.... Second, there are others.... Finally, there are still others...."*	***There are several reasons why a person may do poorly on a test.*** ***First, there is the problem.... Second, there is the problem.... Finally, there is the problem....***
175-76	**Endnote: Questions with Space-filler There**	*Is there a white birch on your property?* *Aren't there good reasons why lumberjacks wear hard hats?*	***Is there a new neighbor on your block?*** ***Aren't there good reasons why lifeguards rope off areas?***
176	**Endnote: Reversal**	*Here comes your brother.*	***Here comes the rain.***

COMMENTS ON THE "ENDNOTES" SECTION [Text, 175-76]

Neither of these endnotes is important for later work in the text, and both are self-explanatory. Their purpose is to anticipate questions that your students might ask.

Sometimes you find sentences—even in the practices—like this one: *The teacher knew that there would be a fire drill.* Notice the word *there* (space-filler *there*) that occupies the subject territory in the dependent clause *that there would be a fire drill.* Note, too, how easy it is to omit the word *there* and replace it with the wording *a fire drill* (the true subject of the verb *would be*): you simply say *The teacher knew that a fire drill would take place [be].*

COMMENTS ON THE "REVIEW" SECTION [Text, 177]

What must be remembered for keeps in this chapter is the content of the Main Subject Test—for Statements; students must especially remember to test wording in the subject territory to see whether the words all sound as if they belong together. As always, the order in which to carry out the tests must be KNOWN and OBSERVED.

FINAL TEST

1. LIST ALL THE TESTS—IN CORRECT ORDER.
2. Write out the TWO ADDED REQUIREMENTS FOR WORDING BETWEEN THE TWO POSITIONS OF A MOVABLE STARTER TO TRULY BE THE MAIN SUBJECT.
3. In a space-filler *there* sentence, how do you find the wording that you must label as main subject?
4. (For bonus credit: Write out as many as you can of the four new meanings that the

verb *be* has when it follows space-filler *there.*)

5. For this passage, CARRY OUT ALL FIVE OF THE TESTS TO FOLLOW TO SUCCEED THAT YOU NOW KNOW—AND IN THE RIGHT ORDER. Make sure that you write out correctly all required do/does/did substitutions as you double underline verbs and that you label correctly all main subject wording.

WINTER DRIVING

Drivers of cars surely must take special precautions in the winter in the mountains. There is no way to predict when the icy roads may be a reason for skidding. Should they use snow tires? They must always use them. They also must choose a front-wheel drive car if they do not wish to keep weights in the rear of their cars. There are forbidding consequences that can befall careless drivers. They most certainly can have bad news in store for themselves. Drivers have even been maimed for life from accidents in icy conditions.

A person who chooses to take curves overfast assuredly will be sorry. Those who pass others too fast also are at risk. There is the chance that this accident could now be one's last.

ANSWERS FOR THE FINAL TEST

1. Main Subject Test—for Questions, Helpers plus WHAT/ING Word Verb Test, Do/does/did Test, Movable Starter Test, Main Subject Test—for Statements
2. The words must sound as if they belong together. The words must be serving as subject of the core verb (answering *WHO* or *WHAT* when asked before it).
3. You look after the verb for the wording that you can substitute for the word *there* in its before-the-verb location (you use the meaning for the verb *be* that fits).
4. *(exist, take place, be at hand, be present)*
5. [must] Ⓢ ^Drivers of cars surely MS must take special precautions in the winter in the mountains. [is] Ⓢ ^There MS is Ⓢ no way to predict when the icy roads may be a reason for skidding. ✓ MS Should Ⓢ [should] they ^ use snow tires? [must] Ⓢ ^They MS must always use them. [must] Ⓢ ^They also MS must choose a front-wheel drive car if they do not wish to keep weights in the rear of their cars. [are] Ⓢ ^There MS are Ⓢ forbidding consequences that can befall careless drivers. [can] Ⓢ ^They most certainly MS can have bad news ✓ in store for themselves. [have] Ⓢ ^Drivers MS have even been maimed for life from accidents in icy conditions.

[will] Ⓢ ^A person who [does choose] ^chooses to take curves overfast assuredly MS will be sorry. ✓ [are] Ⓢ ^Those who [do pass] ^pass others too fast also MS are at risk. [is] Ⓢ ^There MS is Ⓢ the chance that this accident could now be one's last. ✓

POSSIBLE WEIGHTING OF ANSWERS FOR THE FINAL TEST

1. 8% (4% for inclusion of all tests; 4% for listing them in correct order.
2. Each answer is worth 4% (8%).
3. 4%.
4. (Each bonus answer could be worth 2%.)
5. Each of the 56 answers/verb words = 1.43% (56 x 1.43 = 80%).

Chapter 11

Front Wording

Objectives (Items in bolder letters are of greatest importance)

TO LEARN BY MEMORY these items:

Comma Test (to Find Front Adverbials)
Order (revised) for carrying out the tests
How to apply the Main Subject Test—for Questions when a sentence has a front adverbial
How to apply the Movable Starter Test when a sentence has a front adverbial
Rule for punctuating front adverbials

TO LEARN THROUGH EXPERIENCE how to arrange the order of nouns and pronouns

TO APPRECIATE how front adverbials can cause writing to be clearer, more coherent, and more varied

Teaching Helps

CORRECTION (1991 Edition)

Under Ground Rule 3 on page 186, the commentary under the sentence *Carlos, my friend, loaned it to me* should read:

[You **may** say *my friend Carlos loaned it to me.* However, you may **not** say ~~*my friend loaned it to me Carlos.*~~ The word *Carlos* is **not** a front adverbial.]

Note first that the "strike-through" line has been used throughout the text to indicate unacceptable English.

Note secondly that the term FRONT ADVERBIAL is explained on page 183 of the text. Simply, it is WORDING AT THE START OF A SENTENCE THAT IS DOING THE JOB OF AN ADVERB. An example would be the word *later* in the sentence *Later it snowed.*

TEACHING SUGGESTIONS

Truths about Wording in the Front Position: These truths [Text, 178-82] serve as an introduction and orientation to the role of adverbial wording when it starts the sentence.

Ground Rules: These GROUND RULES [Text, 185-87] serve mostly as precautions. They should become instinctive with practice.

Changes Required for the Movable Starter Test: THIS CHANGE [Text, 192-94] CANNOT BE EMPHASIZED ENOUGH WITH STUDENTS. If they forget to carry out this extra step, they are likely to cause confusion for themselves.

Writing Tips for Using Front Adverbials [Text, 201-203]: You may also wish to give students paragraphs to write in which they have a chance to use transitional adverbs and other front adverbials to add coherence, clarity, and interest to their writing. (Be sure to emphasize the importance of the topic sentence—even one with space-filler *there* in it). Topics that require some kind of listing are easiest to implement. These are some examples: Ways to Get Exercise, Ways to Prevent Low Marks, Ways to Help at Home, and so forth.

ALTERNATIVE "EXAMPLES"

Again, here is alternative wording for some of the example material in the text. It can help you introduce the material in a way that is different from the book's.

PAGES	HEADING	EXAMPLES AS IN BOOK	ALTERNATIVE EXAMPLES
179	Truth A	*By the end of summer, we anticipate school.* *After summer, weren't you eager for a change?* *If you have a question, raise your hand.*	***By November, many leaves have fallen.*** ***By Christmas, isn't everyone ready for snow?*** ***If you want good marks, study regularly.***
179	Truth B	*When the halftime arrived, the commercials resumed.* *If you like to read in bed, you must have proper lighting.*	***At every pause in the game, there were more commercials.*** ***If your studying requires concentration, you must turn off the TV.***
179-80	Truth C	*When the sun breaks through the clouds, the brightness causes cheeriness.* *If we speak indistinctly, we can be misunderstood.*	***When there is plenty of rain, there is plenty of growth of vegetation.*** ***When people are truthful, they are courageous.***
180	Truth D	*Occasionally the showers are downpours.* *Perhaps you should exercise more.*	***Yesterday they were unable to practice.*** ***Once there were trolley tracks here.***
181	Truth E	*Due to occasional daydreaming a student can miss important information.* *Almost by chance Mike had offered an invaluable suggestion.*	***Out of respect children should listen to their parents.*** ***As an afterthought she had gone back for her umbrella.***

PAGES	HEADING	EXAMPLES AS IN BOOK	ALTERNATIVE EXAMPLES
181-82	**Truth F**	*Tiny, darting humming birds hover for seconds at a time.* *The Andersons, who are our neighbors, like to go camping.*	***Swift, determined chipmunks scamper after food.*** ***Mr. Mendelson, who is a first-rate carpenter, is changing his profession.***
183	**Labeling for a Front Adverbial**	*Due to the rain, the snow has disappeared.*	***Because of the frost, leaves are beginning to turn color.***
186-87	**Ground Rule 4**	*Occasionally it rains.* *When you smile, you cheer others up.*	***Sometimes roads are closed.*** ***When you lend a hand, you win a friend.***
187	**Ground Rule 5**	*If a student is explaining why his/her work is late, won't a teacher usually listen?*	***If a snowstorm strikes where people are unaccustomed to snow, the effects of the slippery conditions can be disastrous.***
189	**Step 2**	*Because the snow turned to rain, the drifts disappeared.*	***When people use their fireplac-es, heat from the house goes up the chimney too.***
189-90	**Step 2**	*Our plumber, a neighbor's son, does first-rate work.*	***A hawk, a bird that glides, has exceptional eyesight.***
190-91	**Change: Main Subject Test—for Questions**	*If the ground is soft, can a car get stuck?*	***If fresh gravel has been spread, can a car skid?***
192-93	**Change: Movable Starter Test**	*If you are forgetful, you need reminders.*	***If you do math in your head, you do calculations quickly.***
195-97	**Precaution regarding the Main Subject Test—for Statements**	*We seldom discussed the matter.* *Fortunately the sweltering heat has subsided.* *In a minute the phone should ring again.*	***We usually jog in the evening.*** ***Undoubtedly explanations are often just excuses.*** ***In minutes a sunset will fade.***
198	**A Single Switch**	*When winters are too mild, they cause loss of jobs.*	***When droughts last too long, they cause great concern.***
198-99	**A Pair of Switches**	*When my cousin took the driver's test, he failed it.*	***Because Frank studied for the test, he did well on it.***

PAGES	HEADING	EXAMPLES AS IN BOOK	ALTERNATIVE EXAMPLES
199	**More Complicated Switching When Shifting**	*If ants suddenly appear everywhere in a house, they have been forming a nest nearby.* *Ants have been forming a nest near a house if they suddenly appear everywhere in it.*	***If a painting of a seascape matches the colors in a country house, the homeowner might be wise to hang it up anyway.*** ***A country homeowner might be wise to hang up a painting that matches the colors in the house even if it is a seascape.***
200	**Identifying Front Adverbials inside Paragraphs**	*There are many rules that good drivers follow. First, they anticipate problems. For example, when another car slows down without warning, they expect some unpredictable action to take place.*	***There are precautions that gardeners must heed. First, they must buy appropriate seeds. For example, if they plant tomatoes that take longer to grow than the growing season of their region permits, they may never eat their own tomatoes.***
203	**Punctuation Rule for Writing Front Adverbials**	*Provided that you have read the directions carefully, you may proceed to take the test.* *Actually, haven't deer become overabundant lately?* *To check his spelling, he consulted a dictionary.*	***If you work steadily, you should complete a test on time.*** ***In fact, the woods are dangerous during the hunting season.*** ***To test his strength, Pedro did pull-ups.***
204	**Endnote**	*Yesterday, despite the snow, we still had school.*	***Once, after it rained heavily for days, a brook overflowed our driveway.***

Comment on the "Endnotes" Section [Text, 204]

This endnote is helpful for students but will not be referred to again in the text.

Comment on the "Review" Section [Text, 204-205]

These items are WHAT STUDENTS MUST KNOW (relative to the grammatical core of this text): the new order for carrying out the tests, the meaning of the term "front adverbial," and the importance of keeping front adverbial wording out of sight while applying the Main Subject Test—for Questions and the Movable Starter Test.

FINAL TEST

1. LIST ALL THE TESTS—IN CORRECT ORDER.
2. Tell THE ONLY PROOF THAT WORDING IS TRULY SERVING AS A FRONT ADVERBIAL.
3. Tell TWO SITUATIONS DURING WHICH YOU MUST PHYSICALLY COVER FRONT ADVERBIAL WORDING (for bonus credit, add a third).
4. For the passage below, CARRY OUT ALL SIX OF THE TESTS TO FOLLOW TO SUCCEED THAT YOU NOW KNOW—AND IN THE RIGHT ORDER. Make sure that you write out correctly all required do/does/did substitutions as you double underline verbs and that you label correctly all main subject and front adverbial wording.

PROCRASTINATION

A certain father has joint custody with his son over some horses. Would you believe that it was almost a year ago that this father was informed that he must detach wiring from the electrical poles on his property and that he has done nothing about it to this date? If an electrical repairman should get injured on this property, the consequences would certainly be a lawsuit. In such cases, there are laws that protect the electrical company. In your opinion, shouldn't this father have long since taken action?

As it happens, the father is saying to himself: "My son feels that he owns the horses (though he has paid almost nothing either for them or for their upkeep). Therefore, he must be the one who rewires the field."

In contrast, his son uses this reasoning: "Are the odds that great that an electrical repairman will soon come on our property? Isn't it unlikely that even if one did come he would suffer some injury? In light of this, is it really necessary that I exert myself in this case?"

Now you too understand why inertia has prevailed. If you were this parent, would you sell the horses? Maybe you would fix the fencing yourself. If you wanted it done by your son, do you know some secret strategy that you think you could use?

ANSWERS FOR THE FINAL TEST

1. Comma Test, Main Subject Test—for Questions, Helpers plus WHAT/ING Word Verb Test, Do/does/did Test, Movable Starter Test, Main Subject Test—for Statements
2. The front wording can be shifted to the end of the sentence unit with grammatical fit.
3. When testing for a movable starter during (a) the Main Subject Test—for Questions and (b) the Movable Starter Test. (Bonus: when testing for front adverbial wording.)

4. [does] Ⓢ MS [does have] · MS Ⓢ [would]
A certain father has joint custody with his son over some horses. Would you believe that it was almost a
year ago that this father was informed that he must detach wiring from the electrical poles on his property and
FAV
that he has done nothing about it to this date? ⟨If an electrical repairman should get injured on this property,⟩
[would] Ⓢ MS · FAV · [are] Ⓢ MS Ⓢ [do protect]
the consequences would certainly be a lawsuit. ⟨In such cases,⟩ there are laws that protect the electrical company.
FAV MS Ⓢ [should]
⟨In your opinion,⟩ shouldn't this father have long since taken action?
FAV [does happen] [is] Ⓢ MS · [does] Ⓢ MS [does feel] [does own]
⟨As it happens,⟩ the father is saying to himself: "My son feels that he owns the horses (though he has paid
FAV [must] Ⓢ MS [does rewire]
almost nothing either for them or for their upkeep). ⟨Therefore,⟩ he must be the one who rewires the field."
FAV [does] Ⓢ MS [does use] · MS Ⓢ [are]
⟨In contrast,⟩ his son uses this reasoning: "Are the odds that great that an electrical repairman will soon
MS Ⓢ [is] · FAV
come on our property? Isn't it unlikely that even if one did come he would suffer some injury? ⟨In light of this,⟩
MS Ⓢ [is] [do exert]
is it really necessary that I exert myself in this case?"
FAV [do] Ⓢ MS [do understand] · FAV · MS Ⓢ [would]
⟨Now⟩ you too understand why inertia has prevailed. ⟨If you were this parent,⟩ would you sell the horses?
FAV [would] Ⓢ MS · FAV [did want] · MS Ⓢ [do]
⟨Maybe⟩ you would fix the fencing yourself. ⟨If you wanted it done by your son,⟩ do you know some secret
[do think]
strategy that you think you could use?

Possible Weighting of Answers for the Final Test

1. 10% (5% for inclusion of all tests; 5% for listing them in correct order).
2. 5%.
3. Each answer is/could be worth 5% (10%). (The bonus answer could be worth an additional 5%.)
4. Each of the 106 answers (each verb word counts as one answer) is worth .71% [multiply each answer by .71]. (75%) [Note that check marks have NOT been included as required answers, nor will they be in later final tests. You could give bonus credit for these if you wish.]

Chapter 12

Introduction to Conjunctions and Punctuation

Objectives (Items in bolder letters are of greatest importance)

TO LEARN BY MEMORY these terms/items:
- **Series**
- **Predicate**
- **Fragment**
- **Comma splice**
- **List of three coordinating conjunctions**
- **List of nine subordinating conjunctions**
- **Punctuation rule for joining two predicates**
- **Punctuation rule for joining two sentence units**
- **Punctuation rule for separating elements in a minor series**

TO LEARN BY EXPERIENCE these terms/items:
- To recognize and correct fragments, comma splices, and run-on sentences
- A choice of ways to correctly combine sentence units into sentences
- A sense of the role and importance of punctuation marks, especially the period, comma, and semi-colon

Teaching Helps

TEACHING SUGGESTION

Terms to Know [Text, 210-13]: The essence of what students need to know about coordinating and subordinating conjunctions (with respect to the structural goals of this text) is the list of each that is supplied here.

ALTERNATIVE "EXAMPLES"

Again, here is alternative wording for some of the example material in the text. It can help you introduce the material in a way that is different from the book's.

PAGES	HEADING	EXAMPLES AS IN BOOK	ALTERNATIVE EXAMPLES
208-209	Semi-colons That Separate Items in a Series	*School was not called off; the buses arrived late because of the slippery conditions; and all the classes were shortened.*	***An accident had happened; an ambulance and police car were on hand; and traffic was backed up for miles.***

PAGES	HEADING	EXAMPLES AS IN BOOK	ALTERNATIVE EXAMPLES
208-09	**Semi-colons That Separate Items in a Series**	*There are three strategies for writing a report: students can write them out using longhand; they can use a typewriter and add corrections on the good copy; or they can use a computer but not print it out until they have already corrected any mistakes.*	***There are three ways to prevent serious car accidents: drivers can keep a safe distance behind the car in front of them; they can keep their windshields and headlights free of dirt; and they can slow down at the first sign of anything out of the ordinary.***
208-209	**Semi-colons That Serve as Joiners of Sentence Units**	*He works the whole day; he relaxes the whole evening.* *He lost his watch Friday; he found it Sunday.* *He could not open his locker; he had lost the key.*	***He hustles to work; he relaxes on his way home.*** ***A fall sun causes warmth; it causes cheer too.*** ***She bought a new spatula; she had broken the handle on the old one.***
212-13	**Predicate**	*A light snow causes little harm.* *A freezing rain always causes hazardous driving.*	***Extensive flooding causes much grief.*** ***Unmowed fields quickly become overgrown.***
213-14	**The Job of Coordinating Conjunctions**	*Ann and Liz are coming.* *The large box and the small one must come.* *Tom could and should mow the lawn.* *Tom has come and left.* *Joanne spoke and was heard.* *Joanne spoke her mind openly and was respectfully listened to.* *Joanne spoke her mind, and she was heard.* *Joanne spoke to Kelly and me.* *Joanne ran for fun and for exercise.*	***Sherry and Carla will sing.*** ***The wooden chair and the folding one are needed.*** ***We could and should listen better.*** ***We have left and returned.*** ***Susie applied and was accepted.*** ***Susie applied for the job and was offered it.*** ***Susie applied for the job, and she was offered an interview.*** ***Susie told this to Mary and me.*** ***Susie works at a supermarket and for her dad.***

PAGES	HEADING	EXAMPLES AS IN BOOK	ALTERNATIVE EXAMPLES
214	**Telling What a Coordinating Conjunction Joins**	*Sue went to the library and bank.* *Sue went to the library and to the bank.* *Sue went to the library and stayed there.* *Sue went to the library, and she stayed.*	***We walked to the park and a store.*** ***We walked to the park and to a store.*** ***We walked to the park and picnicked there.*** ***We walked to the park, and we ate a picnic supper there.***
215	**Punctuation Rule for Joining Two Predicates**	*The baby could not stand up but could not stay still either.* *Many questions were raised and were answered.* *The teacher sits at his desk or stands by the lectern.*	***The new-born horse could stand but would wobble.*** ***The test was long and was tricky.*** ***A secretary does typing or serves as receptionist.***
215-16	**Punctuation Rule for Joining Two Sentence Units**	*You can send a letter the usual way, or you can send it by "Priority Mail."* *Your answers should be short, and they must be to the point.* *The hill was perfect for sledding, but it was too near a main road.*	***You can vacuum with your glasses on, or you can just vacuum.*** ***You can plan what you write, and then you will write without hesitation.*** ***The birch tree was healthy, but it had a forked trunk.***
216	**Using Conjunctions to Join Elements in a Minor Series**	*Ellen, Donna, and Maria are coming.* *We went, stayed a while, and left.*	***Paco, Sam, and Ned were teammates.*** ***Everyone sang, played some games, and had a good time.***
218	**Combining: Using Just a Semi-colon**	*The snow has melted.* *Winter has stayed.*	***The sun shone brilliantly.*** ***The temperature hovered near zero.***
218	**Combining: Semi-colon + Transitional Adverbial**	*Dad types it. Mom proofreads it.*	***Pens write smoothly. Pencil marks can be erased.***
219	**Combining: Dependent Clause vs. Second Sentence Unit**	*The snow kept falling. It did not amount to much.*	***Summer took too long to come. It provided much needed relaxation.***

PAGES	HEADING	EXAMPLES AS IN BOOK	ALTERNATIVE EXAMPLES
221	Remedying the Fragment	*Though he was not happy at the time.*	***Though he felt tired.***
223	Endnote	*When you shovel a lot of snow, you should use a shovel with a nonstick surface; you should shovel before anyone walks over the path; and you should wear gloves so you do not get frostbite.*	***When winter is approaching, home owners must clean out gutters; they must put snow tires on their cars; and they must turn off any faucets that lead to outdoors.***

Comment on the "Endnote" Section [Text, 223]

The subject matter of this endnote, though useful for mature writers, will not be referred to again in this text.

Comments on the "Review" Section [Text, 223-24]

Students must remember the coordinating and subordinating conjunctions that are listed here. They must also be able to put in practice the three punctuation rules (they should be able to explain the rules so a fellow student can follow their instructions successfully). The new terms for which students should be able to supply an accurate definition or correct examples are: SERIES, PREDICATE, FRAGMENT, and COMMA SPLICE.

Final Test

1. List three coordinating conjunctions.
2. List four subordinating conjunctions (for bonus credit: list the rest).
3. Write out an example of a series.
4. Explain the difference between a predicate and a sentence unit.
5. This passage contains no punctuation and no capital letters. Punctuate the sentences correctly, and add capital letters where they belong.

NEWSPAPERS

newspapers are rich in information they supply up-to-the-minute news and they provide analysis of the causes of events they also have columns by experts who discuss solutions to family community statewide and countrywide problems there are even sections devoted to sports news games and comics

readers of newspapers are of two sorts some browse through the pages one at a time others read the front page and use the index to find what they want to read after that

the page with games can consume most of a person's attention one of these pages can have crossword puzzles and may offer word games called "anagrams" some newspapers even show how experts have played a hand of a game called "bridge"

some people concentrate on the sports pages they read the articles there and they study the statistics to see how their favorite players have done some athletes read these pages to see how their school and others have been ranked others read them to see whether their own achievements have been recorded

other readers go right to the financial pages these readers have invested in stocks bonds or bank certificates they devour the articles and examine any change in the value of their holdings

Answers for the Final Test

1. *and, but, or*
2. *because, since, though, although, until, while, after, before, if* [any four]
3. *trees, bushes, and flowers*
4. A predicate excludes the subject wording that it adds information about; a sentence unit includes both (main) subject wording and its accompanying predicate wording.
5. [Supplied punctuation and capitals are bolded.]

Newspapers

Newspapers are rich in information**.** **T**hey supply up-to-the-minute news**,** and they provide analysis of the causes of events**.** **T**hey also have columns by experts who discuss solutions to family, community**,** statewide**,**[comma is optional] and countrywide problems**.** **T**here are even sections devoted to sports news**,** games**,**[comma is optional] and comics**.**

Readers of newspapers are of two sorts**.** **S**ome browse through the pages one at a time**;** others read the front page [no comma] and use the index after that**.**

The page with games can consume most of a person's attention**.** **O**ne of these pages can have crossword puzzles [no comma] and may offer word games called "anagrams**.**" **S**ome newspapers even show how experts have played a hand of a game called "bridge**.**"

Some people concentrate on the sports pages**.** **T**hey read the articles there**,** and they study the statistics to see how their favorite players have done**.** **S**ome athletes read these pages to see how their school and others have been ranked **while** others read them to see whether their own achievements have been recorded**.**

Other readers go right to the financial pages**.** **T**hese readers have invested in stocks**,** bonds**,**[comma is optional] or bank certificates**.** **T**hey devour the articles [no comma] and closely examine any change in the value of their holdings**.**

Possible Weighting of Answers for the Final Test

1. Each answer is worth 2% (6%).
2. Each answer is worth 1% (4%).
3. 4% (2% for a series; 2% for the punctuation).
4. 6% (3% for each half of the distinction).
4. Each answer is worth 2% (there are 41 answers if you DO count the nonpunctuation of compound predicates as answers and if you do NOT count the optional commas as answers). (82%)

Chapter 13

Questions That Start with a Question Word

Objectives (Items in bolder letters are of greatest importance)

TO **LEARN BY MEMORY** these terms/items:

- **Question-word question**
- **The list of (nine) question words**
- **The difference between statement order and question order (especially after question word wording)**
- **The Expanded Main Subject Test—for Questions**

Teaching Helps

CORRECTION (1991 Edition)

The practices listed on page 242 are in INCORRECT ORDER. Practice K should precede Practices H and J.

TEACHING SUGGESTIONS

Truths about Question Words and Question Word Questions: These truths [Text, 225-35] have special importance because these kinds of questions are so little understood.

Truth G and K [Text, 231-32 and 234–35]**:** The reasons why question-word wording that shifts can be adverbial and yet can **not** be front adverbial wording are twofold. First, this wording cannot shift AS THE SENTENCE STANDS because it would be attempting to ask the question twice at the same time (which is impermissible in English). For example, for the sentence *Where is the wastebasket,* you would be saying ~~*is the wastebasket where*~~.

Second, when a front adverbial comes before a question, it is always followed by a comma. Since the Comma Test always precedes this Main Subject Test—for Questions (Expanded), it stands to reason that the question-word wording that starts the question is not also front adverbial wording. For example, for the sentence *If I may ask again, where is the wastebasket,* the front adverbial is clearly *If I may ask again;* therefore, the wording *where* would not also be a front adverbial.

Truths K and L [Text, 234-35]**:** These are the heart of this expanded test. Take extra time here to be sure that your students realize their differences, how important each is, and that this is the simplest way to tell these two types of questions apart.

Added Practice: Between Practices E and F [Text, 241], you might have students search for and label all verb words inside front adverbials.

In addition, before Practice G [Text, 242], you might give students several question-word questions whose subject is the question-word wording itself. Have your students label just the movable starter and the main subject. Here are some sentences for their practice:

Whose sweater has been left on the chair?
Which birds remain north in winter?
What happened next?
How many people live in Alaska?
What kind of salad dressing appeals to you?
Whose watch alarm just went off?

ALTERNATIVE "EXAMPLES"

Again, here is alternative wording for some of the example material in the text. It can help you introduce the material in a way that is different from the book's.

PAGES	HEADING	EXAMPLES AS IN BOOK	ALTERNATIVE EXAMPLES
225-26	Truth A	*Who came?* *Whom have you called?* *Whose hat is this?*	***Who left?*** ***Whom have they chosen?*** ***Which answer is better?***
225-26	Truth A	*Which day is best?* *When is the play?* *Where have you placed it?* *Why has this happened?* *What do we do next?* *How did you manage that?*	***Which movie did you see?*** ***When is the concert?*** ***Where do you live?*** ***Why has a line formed?*** ***What is on the menu?*** ***How do you tie a slip knot?***
226	Truth B: Example A	*Is your watch gaining time?*	***Can a cloudless day turn to snow?***
227	Truth B: Example B	*What will happen?*	***Who has succeeded?***
228	Truth C	*For how many minutes have you been practicing?*	***On how many quizzes have you gotten 100?***
228	Truth D	*A bike whose tires are soft should not be ridden.* *She speaks when she is called on.* *How we should proceed is unclear.*	***An ax whose edge is dull is unsafe.*** ***Jim knows what he wants to be.*** ***Why they did well is no puzzle to their coach.***
229	Truth E	*Sally has left already.*	***Frank will return soon.***
230	Truth F	*Whose bike has fallen?*	***Which pen writes best?***
231	Truth G	*Whose bike has Carl borrowed?*	***Which pen do you prefer?***
232	Truth H	*Who is coming?* *Whose cup is this?* *At which light should I turn?* *How soon can you come?*	***What happened?*** ***Whose answer is best?*** ***At what time do you eat?*** ***How late has it gotten?***

PAGES	HEADING	EXAMPLES AS IN BOOK	ALTERNATIVE EXAMPLES
233	Truth J	*Who has left?*	***Who would say that?***
234	Truth K	*For how long will it rain?* *How often does the river overflow its banks?*	***For how many minutes must we stall?*** ***How often does your mom bake a pie?***
235	Truth L	*Which tree has lost its branch?* *Whose quarter fell through the grate?*	***Whose paper has just fallen?*** ***Which trees grow best in this region?***
237-38	Step I	*How early we should leave has not been decided.*	***Which questions we should answer is not clear.***
239-41	Steps III,B,2	*If you were building a fire, what size branches would you choose?*	***If you wanted to save electricity, where would you start?***
241-42	Steps III,B,2,b	*When you voted, who became president of the class?*	***In yesterday's debate, which side won?***
242	Endnote	*He has not refused nor will he.*	***He has not quit nor will he.***

COMMENT ON THE "ENDNOTES" SECTION [Text, 242]

This is simply a point of interest. The word *nor* is another of the one-word coordinating conjunctions.

COMMENT ON THE "REVIEW" SECTION [Text, 243-44]

The items that students MUST KNOW BY HEART are: the list of question words, the difference between starter-verb questions and question-word questions, the difference between statement order and question order, and how this EXPANDED TEST works (they must be able to write out, in their own words, all the STEPS of the TEST).

FINAL TEST

1. WRITE OUT FOUR OF THE NINE QUESTION WORDS. (Bonus credit: add the other five).
2. EXPLAIN THE DIFFERENCE BETWEEN A STARTER-VERB QUESTION AND A QUESTION-WORD QUESTION.
3. Create a STATEMENT ORDER QUESTION that starts with these two words: *Which store.*
4. Write out the SUBJECT of the sentence that you just wrote.
5. Create a QUESTION ORDER QUESTION that starts with these two words: *Which store.*
6. Write out the SUBJECT of the sentence that you just wrote.
7. WHAT KIND OF WORD MARKS THE BEGINNING OF THE (REST OF THE) SENTENCE AFTER QUESTION-WORD WORDING?
8. For the passage below, CARRY OUT ALL SIX OF THE TESTS TO FOLLOW TO SUCCEED THAT YOU NOW KNOW—AND IN THE RIGHT ORDER. Make sure that you write out

correctly all required do/does/did substitutions as you double underline verbs and that you label correctly all main subject, question-word question, and front adverbial wording.

FIRE DRILLS

How many fire drills take place at your house? Hopefully the record at your house is better than the record at ours. Some years ago, my father did buy fire-escape ladders. How recently do you suppose that my parents last tried a fire drill? When one of my sisters was in a room that she has not occupied for seven years, they held their last fire drill.

Why has our family held so few drills? Would your parents hold many fire drills if they never remove their storm windows even in summer? In addition, which window opens easily enough that younger children could easily open it by themselves? If I were to ask you, would any of you believe that we have now been using wood fires to heat our house for over five years?

In people's lives, they can neglect certain activities that in time they might greatly regret.

ANSWERS FOR THE FINAL TEST

1. *Who, whose, whom, which, when, where, why, what, how*
2. The first word of a starter verb question must be a starter helping verb; the first word of a question word question will either be a question word or will be part of question word wording.
3. *Which store has pen-size flashlights?*
4. *Which store.*
5. *Which store will we go to first?*
6. *We.*
7. A verb word (which either is or contains the movable starter).
8. [How many fire drills](S) ^take [do take] (MS) place at your house? ⟨Hopefully,⟩(FAV) ^[the record at your house](S) is [is] (MS) better ✓ than the record at ours. ⟨Some years ago,⟩(FAV) ^[my father](S) did buy [did] (MS) fire-escape ladders. ⟨How recently⟩ do (MS) [you](S) ^suppose [do] that my parents last ^tried [did try] a fire drill? ⟨When one of my sisters was in a room that she has not occupied for seven years,⟩(FAV) ^[they](S) [did] (MS) ^held [did hold] their last fire drill.

⟨Why⟩ has (MS) [our family](S) ^held [has] so few drills? Would (MS) [your parents](S) ^hold [would] many fire drills if they never ^remove [do remove] their storm windows even in summer? ⟨In addition,⟩(FAV) [which window](S) ^opens [does open] (MS) easily enough that younger children could easily open it by themselves? ⟨If I were to ask you,⟩(FAV) would (MS) [any of you](S) ^believe [would] that we have now been using wood fires to heat our house for over five years?

⟨In people's lives,⟩(FAV) ^[they](S) can neglect [can] (MS) certain activities that in time they might greatly regret.

POSSIBLE WEIGHTING OF ANSWERS FOR THE FINAL TEST

1. Each answer is worth 1% (4%).
2. Each answer is worth 3% (6%).
3. 3%; 4. 2%; 5. 3%; 6. 2%; 7. 2%
8. Each answer/verb word—and label for movable starters too—is worth 1.26% [multiply each of the 62 answers by 1.26] (78%).

Chapter 14

Subjects versus Objects

Objectives (Items in bolder letters are of greatest importance)

TO LEARN BY MEMORY these terms/items:
- **Object of verb**
- **Object of preposition**
- **Prepositional phrase**
- **Nonmain subject**
- **Nonmovable starter**
- **The list of nine prepositions**
- **The order of the tests**
- **The order of the PARTS of Test 7**

TO LEARN BY EXPERIENCE the correct spelling of pronouns as subjects and as objects

TO BECOME ACQUAINTED WITH the terms "transitive verb" and "intransitive verb"

Teaching Helps

COMMENTS ON THE *SKILLS PRACTICE BOOK* AND *ANSWER BOOK*

If students make a mistake in finding the whole object of preposition when these include a noun and a following prepositional phrase that is modifying it, it is a minor mistake in this chapter. You could overlook such mistakes in your grading, especially for classes with lower ability.

COMMENT ON THE DEFINITION OF OBJECT OF VERB (1991 EDITION)

A more accurate definition of an OBJECT OF VERB [Text, 248] would be: **The wording that answers *WHOM* or *WHAT* when asked after any verb (other than *be* or a verb that the verb *be* can replace—see endnotes in this chapter and the next).**

TEACHING SUGGESTION

Truths [Text, 245–62]: These truths make important points that are indispensable as background for success with the PARTS of this TEST.

ALTERNATIVE "EXAMPLES"

Again, here is alternative wording for some of the example material in the text. It can help you introduce the material in a way that is different from the book's.

PAGES	HEADING	EXAMPLES AS IN BOOK	ALTERNATIVE EXAMPLES
245-46	**Truth A**	*_______ found a toy.* *The boy found _______.* *The boy came with _______.*	***_______ lifted the stone.*** ***Jake lifted _______.*** ***Jake left with _______.***
246	**Truth B**	*Bill broke the bat.* *He studies for an hour.* *Bill lacks the time.* *Bill came with friends.*	***Julie cut her finger.*** ***We stayed at the library.*** ***Julie owns a computer.*** ***Julie stood by the door.***
249	**Truth D**	*Because Joe had misplaced his watch* *When the cold spell would pass couldn't be forecast.*	***Though Bart missed a class*** ***When he would take charge of his studies was the question.***
251	**Labeling for Noun-Job Wording by Job**	*Joe is heading for home because he left his homework there.*	***Jill is going to the store because her mother needs more milk.***
252-53/ 254	**Truth B**	*When the phone rings, someone should answer it.*	***When indoor plants are not watered, they wither.***
254-55	**Test 7, Part A**	*Pedro will come if he is able to.*	***We cannot begin until all the supplies arrive.***
255	**Transitive Verb**	*Sue broke her necklace.*	***Jeff found his watch.***
255	**Intransitive Verb**	*Cats move quietly.*	***Clouds can move quickly.***
256	**Truth C**	*Whenever Paul used his favorite bat, he knew that he could get a hit.*	***Whenever Jen wore her favorite dress, she knew that everyone would like it.***
256-57	**Truth D**	*Ed arrived after the bell.* *Who lives on Houston Street?* *Larry went by car.* *We exercise for our health.*	***The package arrived on Friday.*** ***We are going to the pizza place.*** ***We went on foot.*** ***We went for the exercise.***
257	**Truth E**	*He put his knapsack on the ground.* *Ed saw me in the corridor today.*	***He found a quarter on the sidewalk.*** ***We heard a noise in the wall yesterday.***

II-14: Subjects versus Objects

PAGES	HEADING	EXAMPLES AS IN BOOK	ALTERNATIVE EXAMPLES
258	**Test 7, Part B**	*We placed the tent on high ground.* *Everyone knows when the last day of school is.*	***We parked our car near the exit.*** ***Mountain climbers know that trees are shorter at higher altitudes.***
259	**Truth B**	*Maria came with a friend.* *George came with his tools.*	***Mary Lou came with her sister.*** ***The hunters left with their guns.***
260	**Truth C**	*George went to the shore for a week.*	***We sat on the porch for an hour.***
260	**Truth D**	*Janice went to the store.* *Janice went to the store by the gas station.* *Janice went to the store by the gas station with the lowest prices.* *Janice went to the store by the gas station with the lowest prices yesterday.*	***We looked for a house.*** ***We looked for a house with a fence.*** ***We looked for a house with a fence on a dead-end street.*** ***We looked for a house with a fence on a dead-end street yesterday.***
261	**Truth E**	*The deer disappeared into the woods.* *I found the book of my brother.*	***The watering can sat on the window sill.*** ***I can hear the phone of my neighbor.***
264	**Test 7, Part D**	*We arrived at the tower at the top of the mountain at midday.*	***We met at the entrance of the store by the gas station at three.***
266-67	**Case**	*I know that we will succeed.* *She asked whether we were coming.* *Al said to Jane and me that the book was for her.* *When we throw sticks for our dog, he brings them to us.* *Who knows who is coming?* *Al asked to whom he should send them.*	***I knew that we would be early.*** ***She wondered what they had decided.*** ***Gus said to Ruth and me that the call was for her.*** ***When we write away for things, the mailman brings them to us.*** ***Who could have guessed who would win.*** ***We wondered for whom the ad was intended.***

PAGES	HEADING	EXAMPLES AS IN BOOK	ALTERNATIVE EXAMPLES
267	**Indirect Objects**	*Harry gave the dog a bone.*	***I sent my cousin a letter.***
268	**Predicate Noun**	*Brian was the captain.* *Sheila was a cheerleader.* *Joanne became the president.*	***Bert was the president.*** ***Sally was the treasurer.*** ***Will became an auto mechanic.***
268	**Noun in Apposition**	*Fred, my brother, has left.*	***Rascal, my dog, carries a twig as a ritual.***

Comment on the "Endnotes" Section [Text, 267-69]

The treatment of indirect objects, predicate nouns, and nouns in apposition has been relegated to endnotes so that the concepts of object of verb and object of preposition can become as deeply rooted as possible (at this introductory level). Students are not required to identify any of these three elements in their practice work.

Comments on the "Review" Section [Text, 269-70]

There has been enough repetition built into this chapter that students should be able to write out the following (at least in their own words): the strategies for finding nonmain subjects, objects of verbs, and objects of prepositions; the order of the PARTS of this test; the new order of the tests; and what a prepositional phrase is. They must not forget these. They must also have memorized the nine prepositions listed here.

Final Test

1. LIST ALL THE TESTS—IN CORRECT ORDER.
2. EXPLAIN EXACTLY WHERE A NONMAIN SUBJECT IS LOCATED.
3. EXPLAIN THE STRATEGY FOR FINDING OBJECTS OF VERBS.
4. LIST ALL NINE OF THE CHIEF PREPOSITIONS.
5. EXPLAIN THE STRATEGY FOR FINDING OBJECTS OF PREPOSITIONS.
6. WRITE OUT THE ORDER IN WHICH TO CARRY OUT THE "PARTS" OF THE NOUN JOB TESTS.
7. For the passage below, CARRY OUT ALL SEVEN OF THE TESTS TO FOLLOW TO SUCCEED THAT YOU NOW KNOW—AND IN THE RIGHT ORDER. Make sure that you write out correctly all required do/does/did substitutions as you double underline verbs and that you label correctly all main subject, question-word question, and front adverbial wording. Finally, be sure to label correctly all nonmain subjects, objects of verbs, prepositions, and objects of prepositions.

A LABORATORY RAT

At Thanksgiving time my son brought a rat home for the purpose of some psychology experiments. [Since he would not be returning this rat], he made a large cage for it.

How long would you guess [that (=clause introducer) this rat of his remained in its cage]? Would any self-respecting rat [that (=clause introducer) you know] prefer a cage to freedom? [If you can believe it], this misplaced laboratory rat had the run of the basement of our house for two days.

Answers for the Final Test

1. Comma Test, Main Subject Test—for Questions, Helpers plus WHAT/ING Word Verb Test, Do/does/did Test, Movable Starter Test, Main Subject Test—for Statements, Noun Job Tests
2. You find a nonmain subject between a nonmovable starter and the introducer of a clause (whether visible or suppliable); it answers *WHO* or *WHAT* when asked there. (You could give bonus credit for mentioning the introducer too.)
3. You find objects of verbs by looking for the wording that answers *WHOM* or *WHAT* when asked after a (final) verb word.
4. *from, with, in; on, by, for; at, to, of*
5. You find objects of prepositions by looking for the wording that answers *WHOM* or *WHAT* when asked after a preposition.
6. Nonmain subjects, objects of verbs, prepositions, objects of prepositions
7. FAV ⟨At (OP) Thanksgiving time⟩, [did] Ⓢ my son (MS) [did bring] brought (OV) a rat home for (OP) the purpose of (OP) some psychology experiments.

FAV ⟨[Since (S) he would not be returning (OV) this rat],⟩ [did] Ⓢ he (MS) [did make] made (OV) a large cage for (OP) it.

⟨How long⟩ (MS) would Ⓢ you [would] guess (OV) [that (S) this rat of (OP) his [did remain] remained in (OP) its cage]? (MS) Would Ⓢ any self-respecting rat [that (S) you [do know] know] [would] prefer (OV) a cage to (OP) freedom? FAV ⟨[If (S) you can believe (OV) it],⟩ [did] Ⓢ this misplaced laboratory rat [did have] had (OV) the run of (OP) the basement of (OP) our house for (OP) two days.

Possible Weighting of Answers for the Final Test

1. 6% (3% or ½ each for inclusion of all the tests and 3% or ½ each for listing them in correct order).
2. 6%.
3. 6%.
4. 10% (1 each plus 1 if all nine).
5. 6%.
6. 6% (3% for inclusion of all the PARTS and 3% for listing them in correct order).
7. 60% (.95% for each correct answer; there are 63 answers—multiply each by .95).

Chapter 15

Adjectives

Objectives (Items in bolder letters are of greatest importance)

TO LEARN BY MEMORY these terms/items:
- **The list of articles**
- **The order in which to carry out the tests**
- **The questions that adjectives answer**
- **The STEPS of the Adjective Test—in correct order** (in their own words)
- **The seven Spelling Rules** (in their own words)

TO LEARN BY EXPERIENCE:
- Where, primarily, to find adjectives and where to find phrases and clauses that do the job of an adjective
- What a noun cluster is
- How adjectives answer the questions of an adjective

Teaching Helps

Wording Correction (1991 Edition)

On page 276, the wording of the title of Practice B should read: **"Finding adjectives inside noun clusters"** (NOT "inside noun clauses"). The wording is correct in the *Skills Practice Book.*

Comments on the *Skills Practice Book* and *Answer Book*

In the *Skills Practice Book* [Skills, 159], the first word on line 2 (in the third paragraph of Practice M) is *much.* This has NOT been identified as an adjective in the *Answer Book* (see page 74) because, though it is sayable with *time,* it seems to modify the word *more* instead, which would make it an adverb. Note that it is sayable with *more* and answers some question before it. This is a rare occurrence.

Teaching Suggestions

Truths about Adjectives [Text, 271–77] **and Truths about Noun Clusters** [Text, 278–81]: These truths are especially important not only because they are the foundation for the chapter but especially because, in some instances, they serve as the instruction of the chapter as well.

Spelling Rules: These rules [Text, 289–92] are often usage rules—and the ones most violated by students. They deserve your students' fullest attention.

Writing Tips for Using Hyphens and Irregular Comparisons: These rules [Text, 293] are treated almost as endnotes here; they are a little aside from the central focus of this introductory-level book.

Rules for Agreement of a Verb with Its Subject: You can teach these rules [Text, 293 and 327–29] at any time from this point on. Half of them depend on the instruction of this chapter as their base.

ALTERNATIVE "EXAMPLES"

Again, here is alternative wording for some of the example material in the text. It can help you introduce the material in a way that is different from the book's.

PAGES	HEADING	EXAMPLES AS IN BOOK	ALTERNATIVE EXAMPLES
271	**Truth A**	*Two trees* *Tall trees* *Maple trees* *Pretty trees*	***Two apples*** ***Large apples*** ***McIntosh apples*** ***Red apples***
272	**Truth B**	*Homeowners keep pets.* *Nearby homeowners* *Fayetteville's homeowners* *Countless homeowners* *Country homeowners*	***Drivers drive safely.*** ***Certain drivers*** ***Portland's drivers*** ***Many drivers*** ***Handicapped drivers***
273	**Truth C**	*The two tall pretty maple trees are on my property.*	***The beautiful new red Ford Escort belongs to our neighbor.***
273	**Truth D**	*large books / books available* *red ones / something new*	***stone walls / walls nearby*** ***small ones / everything left***
274	**Truth E**	*One worthwhile book mentioned was the* Bible.	***One affordable magazine offered was* Home Office.**
274	**Truth F**	*High, racing, fleecy clouds passed overhead.*	***Spectacular, ever-changing, inspiring sunsets do occasionally occur.***
274-75	**Truth G**	*Beth owns several rather rare stamps.*	***Barbara owns several rather pretty dresses.***
276	**Truth H**	*The room with a carpet has a beige tone.* *The toy of the child has fallen.*	***The dog on the chain barks a lot.*** ***The cry of a baby is easy to hear.***
277	**Truth J**	*The room that is carpeted has a beige tone.* *The toy that the child owns has fallen.*	***The dog that is chained barks a lot.*** ***The crying that a baby does is easy to hear.***
278	**Truth A**	*An uneven surface has drawbacks.* *A short answer was requested.* *The snow fell heavily.*	***An A is never a gift.*** ***A spring can supply abundant water.*** ***The answer was on the mark.***

PAGES	HEADING	EXAMPLES AS IN BOOK	ALTERNATIVE EXAMPLES
279	Truth B	*January can bring the song of birds.*	***A passing truck can cause the barking of a dog.***
280-81	Truth C	*The cost of the toy had risen.* *He did not know the cost of the toy.* *He knew of the cost of the toy.* *several old books of value*	***The cost of paper has increased.*** ***I dislike the cost of paper.*** ***I have just learned of the cost of paper.*** ***some new stamps of interest***
283-84	Step 1	*International Business Machines sells computers outside the United States of America.* *Des Moines is the capital of Iowa.*	***Minnesota Mining and Manufacturing Company sells its products in Great Britain.*** ***Salt Lake City is the capital of Utah.***
284-85	Step 1b	*The friendly little kitten*	***The smart young dog***
286	Step 1d	*the Westbrook school building*	***the Livingston bus station***
286-87	Step 2	*Nothing particular* *Somewhere nearby*	***Everything worthwhile*** ***Everywhere possible***
289	**Spelling Rule for *A/An***	*A book* *A large apple* *A used book* *An apple* *An open book* *An hour*	***A gain*** ***A blue notebook*** ***A useful gadget*** ***An ending*** ***An equal chance*** ***An honest answer***
290	**Spelling Rule for *Its***	*Its location* *Its meaning* *Its duration*	***Its purpose*** ***Its appearance*** ***Its nature***
290	***Their/ They're/ There***	*Their pens* *Their belongings* *Their answers*	***Their watches*** ***Their homes*** ***Their coats***
291	**Spelling Rule for Apostrophe plus *S* or Just an Apostrophe**	*families' houses* *workers' union* *ships' sails* *George's* *family's* *children's*	***leaders' remarks*** ***cities' planners*** ***trees' leaves*** ***Paula's*** ***child's*** ***woman's***

PAGES	HEADING	EXAMPLES AS IN BOOK	ALTERNATIVE EXAMPLES
291-92	**Spelling Rule for Comparing Two of a Kind**	*Bill is faster than Mike.* *Volleyball is easier than lacrosse.* *The bus is later than usual today.*	***Planes are faster than trains.*** ***Swimming is easier than running.*** ***Will is wiser than his brother.***
292	**Spelling Rule for Comparing Three or More of a Kind**	*Bill is the fastest in his family.* *English is my easiest subject.* *Summer is the warmest season.*	***Michelle is the smartest in our class.*** ***Math is my easiest subject.*** ***Winter is the coldest season.***
292	**Spelling Rule for Using *More* Or *-Er***	*That is prettier. / That is more pretty.* *He is happier now. / He is more happy now.*	***Oaks are heartier. / Oaks are more hearty.*** ***The baby is noisier. / The baby is more noisy.***
293	**Hyphens/ Compari-sons**	*This has far–reaching importance.*	***Some medicines have long–lasting effects.***
293	**Endnote: Predicate Adjectives**	*My brother is tall.* *My brother seems tall.* *My brother is tall.* *Bill is tall.* *It is tall.*	***My marks are respectable.*** ***My marks seem respectable.*** ***My sister is generous.*** ***Eileen is pretty.*** ***It is fragile.***

COMMENT ON THE "ENDNOTES" SECTION [Text, 293–294]

I feel that it would be counterproductive for students to spend more time than this on predicate adjectives at this introductory level.

COMMENTS ON THE "REVIEW" SECTION [Text, 294–97]

The "memory" expected of students from this chapter is to be able to list the articles and the order of the steps and to explain the following in their own words: the STEPS of the Adjective Test itself (and in correct order), the Spelling Rules, and the term "keyword." Students should also be able to identify which question an adjective is answering when they are given an example of one in context.

FINAL TEST

1. WRITE OUT THE MAIN PARTS OF THE FIVE STEPS OF THE ADJECTIVE TEST—AND IN CORRECT ORDER.

2. WRITE OUT TWO OF THE QUESTIONS THAT ADJECTIVES CAN ANSWER. For bonus credit: Add the other two.
3. LIST ALL ARTICLES.
4. EXPLAIN THE IMPORTANCE OF A KEYWORD.
5. EXPLAIN HOW YOU KNOW WHETHER A WORD IS A NOUN. INCLUDE BOTH STRATEGIES.
6. EXPLAIN HOW YOU KNOW WHETHER A WORD IS AN ADJECTIVE. GIVE EITHER STRATEGY. For bonus credit: explain both strategies.
7. For the passage below, CARRY OUT ALL EIGHT OF THE TESTS TO FOLLOW TO SUCCEED THAT YOU NOW KNOW—AND IN THE RIGHT ORDER. Make sure that you write out correctly all required do/does/did substitutions as you double underline verbs and that you label correctly all main subject, question-word question, and front adverbial wording. Finally, be sure to label correctly all nonmain subjects, objects of verbs, prepositions, objects of prepositions, articles, nouns, keyword pronouns, adjectives, and prepositional phrases that are doing the job of an adjective.

DIFFERENCES IN TEMPERATURE

[When my older brother was driving to work in the rain recently], he started skidding [before he reached the end of our road]. What temperature was showing on the bank's thermometer in town? That reliable thermometer showed a temperature of thirty-five degrees. How could an unsuspecting person have skidded in above-freezing temperatures? Obviously the temperature of the air by our house could not have matched the temperature in the center of town. Mustn't everyone sensible then drive more carefully on roads in country places [if it is raining at near-freezing temperatures]?

ANSWERS FOR THE FINAL TEST

1. (a) Apply the THE Test and the Capital Letter Test to find all keyword nouns; (b) Label every keyword pronoun; (c) Label all articles; (d) Label all adjectives; (e) Label all clauses/phrases that do the job of an adjective.
2. *Which, whose, how many/(much), what kind of*
3. *An, a, the*
4. The keyword is the noun or pronoun in a noun cluster that an article sometimes announces and that adjectives modify (are sayable with/answer some question about).
5. (a) It is capitalized and serving as keyword inside a noun territory. (b) You can say *the* in front of it outside the sentence (the two words must sound right together and the dictionary meaning must not change); and it is serving as keyword inside a noun territory.
6. You can say it with the keyword, or it answers the question of an adjective when you ask the question in front of the keyword.

7. ⟨[When my older brother was driving to work in the rain recently],⟩ [did] he [did start] started skidding [before he [did reach] reached the end of our road]. What temperature was showing on the bank's thermometer in town? [did] That reliable thermometer [did show] showed a temperature of thirty-five degrees. ⟨How⟩ could an unsuspecting person [could] have skidded in above-freezing temperatures? ⟨Obviously⟩ [couldn't] the temperature of the air by our house could not have matched the temperature in the center of town. Mustn't everyone sensible then [must] drive more carefully on roads in country places [if it is raining at near-freezing temperatures]?

[I have considered it OPTIONAL for students to place a dotted bracket over keywords before adjectival phrases and clauses. Note that *skidding* is a noun because it does respond to the THE Test. The prepositional phrase *in town* is doing the job of an adjective because it is modifying *bank;* this is so tricky that I would accept any student answer as correct.]

Possible Weighting of Answers for the Final Test

1. 9% (5% for including all parts; 4% for listing them in correct order).
2. 4% (2% each).
3. 2% (two thirds of a percent for each).
4. 4%.
5. 8% (4% for each strategy).
6. 5%.
7. 68% (127 answers x .54 each).

Chapter 16

Adverbs

Objectives (Items in bolder letters are of greatest importance)

TO LEARN BY MEMORY:
The questions answered by adverbs
The order in which to carry out the tests
The Adverb Test
The three Spelling Rules (in their own words)

TO LEARN BY EXPERIENCE:
Where to find adverbs
Where to find phrases and clauses that do the job of an adverb
How adverbs answer the questions of an adverb

Teaching Helps

TEACHING SUGGESTIONS

Truths about Adverbs That Modify Verbs and about Adverbs That Modify Adjectives and Other Adverbs [Text, 298–306]**:** These truths, just like those in the chapter on adjectives, have extra importance because they serve both as the foundation for the chapter and, in some instances, as the instruction of the chapter at the same time.

Spelling Rules [Text, 307-309]**:** These are usage rules that you will want your students to make their own.

ALTERNATIVE "EXAMPLES"

Again, here is alternative wording for some of the example material in the text. It can help you introduce the material in a way that is different from the book's.

PAGES	HEADING	EXAMPLES AS IN BOOK	ALTERNATIVE EXAMPLES
299	**Truth A**	*He walks slowly.* *He often takes a walk.* *He does not know the answer.* *He found the book quickly.* *Suddenly, the sun brightened everything.*	***She talks quickly.*** ***She often speaks out.*** ***She does not dislike a debate.*** ***She found her watch quickly.*** ***Fortunately, she remembered where she had left it.***

PAGES	HEADING	EXAMPLES AS IN BOOK	ALTERNATIVE EXAMPLES
299-300	Truth B	*He put it there.* *He came late.* *He left deliberately.* *It moved rapidly.* *It reappeared unexpectedly.* *He wins occasionally.* *He will return shortly.*	***He put it here.*** ***He came Sunday.*** ***He left deliberately.*** ***It moved haltingly.*** ***It reappeared unexpectedly.*** ***He wins sometimes.*** ***He will return soon.***
300-01	Truth C	*Now Al has lost his pen.* *Al now has lost his pen.* *Al has now lost his pen.* *Al has lost his pen now.* *Al has lost his pen again now.*	***Now we have found a bargain.*** ***We now have found a bargain.*** ***We have now found a bargain.*** ***We have found a bargain now.*** ***We have found a bargain again now.***
301	Truth D	*Undoubtedly, he did not stay long there yesterday deliber-ately.*	***Reportedly, he did not wait long there yesterday happily.***
301-02	Truth E	*Unfortunately, he could not put the note there immediately yesterday.*	***Hopefully, he will not mail the book back there immediately.***
303	Truth F	*He put it on the shelf.* *He came at noon.* *It moved with great speed.* *It reappeared with no warning.* *He wins on occasion.* *He will return in no time.*	***He put it in the drawer.*** ***He came at dusk.*** ***It moved with little difficulty.*** ***It reappeared with no warning.*** ***He wins with frequency.*** ***He will return in an hour.***
304	Truth G	*He put it where he could find it.* *He came when he could get free.* *He left because he was late.* *It moved as a steam roller would.* *It reappeared though it had not been expected.* *He wins whenever he gets lucky.* *He will return when he has fin-ished lunch.*	***He put it where it was safe.*** ***He came when he needed help.*** ***He left because he was needed.*** ***It moved as an ant would.*** ***It reappeared though it had vanished.*** ***He wins whenever he chooses.*** ***He will return when he has found what he needs.***
304-05	Truth A	*rather distant rumble / drives too quickly* *especially strong magnet / vis-its fairly often*	***rather faint sound / phones too seldom*** ***unusually strong wind / jogs quite quickly***
306	Note	*That put me somewhat at an advantage.*	***He aimed directly at the bee's nest.***

PAGES	HEADING	EXAMPLES AS IN BOOK	ALTERNATIVE EXAMPLES
308	Spelling Rule for Using Too Right	*Louise came too.* *She writes neatly too.* *Everyone arrived too early.* *He speaks too quickly.* *We have too little time.* *You cannot have too many spare pens.*	***Mark stayed too.*** ***Mark works hard too.*** ***A few arrived too late.*** ***Some answer too hurriedly.*** ***We have too many tests.*** ***We have too little time.***
309	Examples	*He has a loud laugh. / He laughs loudly.* *He has a regular job. / He wears jeans regularly.* *He has a rapid gait. / He walks rapidly.* *Dan is a good student / Dan studies well.* *Juan has a good bat. / Juan bats well.* *Emily has good clothes. / Emily dresses well.*	***She has clear thoughts. / She thinks clearly.*** ***She wears different clothes. / She dresses differently.*** ***She has an awkward throw. / She throws awkwardly.*** ***Doug is a good typist. / Doug types well.*** ***Bonnie is a good planner. / Bonnie plans well.*** ***Rover is a good jumper. / Rover jumps well.***
310	End-notes: vs. Prepositions	*No one went in.* *We just stood by.* *He just went on.* *He then came to.*	***We just went in.*** ***Everyone stood by.*** ***The conversation went on.*** ***She quickly came to.***
310	End-notes: as Modifiers of Sentence Units	*The phone does not ring often.*	***We do not cook out often.***

COMMENTS ON THE "ENDNOTES" SECTION [Text, 310–11]

The first endnote is important if students are to avoid confusion in a few of the exercises of the text.

The second and third endnotes are more matters of interest that will not be referred to again.

COMMENTS ON THE "REVIEW" SECTION [Text, 311–12]

Students should be able to identify which question an adverb is answering when they are given an example of one in context. In addition, they should be able to list all the TESTS in correct order; and they should be able to explain in their own words the Adverb Test and the three Spelling Rules.

FINAL TEST

1. LIST ALL THE TESTS—IN CORRECT ORDER.
2. WRITE OUT THREE OF THE QUESTIONS THAT ADVERBS CAN ANSWER. For bonus credit: Add three more.
3. EXPLAIN ONE WAY IN WHICH ADVERBS DIFFER FROM ADJECTIVES. For bonus credit: explain two additional ways.
4. EXPLAIN HOW YOU CAN TELL WHETHER A PREPOSITIONAL PHRASE IS DOING THE JOB OF AN ADVERB OR ADJECTIVE.
5. For the passage below, CARRY OUT ALL NINE OF THE TESTS TO FOLLOW TO SUCCEED THAT YOU NOW KNOW—AND IN THE RIGHT ORDER. Make sure that you write out correctly all required do/does/did substitutions as you double underline verbs and that you label correctly all main subject, question-word question, and front adverbial wording. Finally, be sure to label correctly all nonmain subjects, objects of verbs, prepositions, objects of prepositions, articles, nouns, adjectives, keywords, adverbs, and prepositional phrases (according to the job each is doing).

BASKETBALL CAMP

At the request of his coach, my brother went to basketball camp in the summer. In the past he would sometimes excel at basketball [because he has a rather unusual amount of natural talent].

Now he quite quickly takes charge in every game. Surefootedly, he dribbles to the opponent's court. On arrival he deftly passes the ball to a racing teammate. On occasions, he dribbles right to the basket. Unfortunately, he needs improvement in his shooting ability still. On the other hand, he does not need any improvement in his dribbling ability [since he has already mastered this skill].

ANSWERS FOR THE FINAL TEST

1. Comma Test, Main Subject Test—for Questions, Helpers plus WHAT/ING Word Verb Test, Do/does/did Test, Movable Starter Test, Main Subject Test—for Statements, Noun Job Tests, Adjective Test, Adverb Test
2. *how, when, where, why, how often, under what circumstances*
3. The "position" of adverbs is virtually anywhere; the "position" of adjectives is inside a noun cluster. The questions answered by adverbs differ from the questions answered by adjectives—also where you ask the questions differs. Adverbs are "sayable with"—that is, modify—verbs (as well as verbs plus their companion wording and/or modifiers), adjectives, and other adverbs; adjectives are sayable with nouns and pronouns.
4. In the same way that you can tell adverbs from adjectives [see No. 3]. A distinctive feature of adjective phrases and clauses is that they can only follow the keyword noun or pronoun that they modify.

5. At the request of his coach, my brother went to basketball camp in the summer. In the past he would sometimes excel at basketball [because he has a rather unusual amount of natural talent]. Now he quite quickly takes charge in every game. Surefootedly, he dribbles to the opponent's court. On arrival he deftly passes the ball to a racing teammate. On occasions, he dribbles right to the basket. Unfortunately, he needs improvement in his shooting ability still. On the other hand, he does not need any improvement in his dribbling ability [since he has already mastered this skill].

[The "FAV" label (for "front adverbial") is sufficient to identify an adverb or adverbial phrase or clause that starts a sentence as adverbial in function.]

Possible Weighting of Answers for the Final Test

1. 8% (4% or ½% each for inclusion of all the tests and 4% or ½% each for listing them in correct order).
2. 6% (2% for each correct answer).
3. 6% (3% for a correct answer for adverbs; 3% for a correct answer for adjectives).
4. 6% (3% for a correct answer for adverbs; 3% for a correct answer for adjectives).
5. 74% (.463 for each correct answer; there are 160 answers).

Chapter 17

Introduction to Dependent Clauses

Objectives (Items in bolder letters are of greatest importance)

TO LEARN BY MEMORY:

The (revised) order in which to carry out the tests

The Dependent Clause Test

TO RECOGNIZE THESE WORDS AS DEPENDENT CLAUSE INTRODUCERS:

The word *that*

The nine dependent clause introducers that have been listed

The nine question words

TO LEARN BY EXPERIENCE:

The ingredients and functions of dependent clauses

The functions of dependent clause introducers

Teaching Helps

WORDING CORRECTION (1991 Edition)

Under the **"Order in Which to Carry out the Tests,"** page 323, the eighth entry should read: **"DEPENDENT CLAUSE TEST"** (NOT "Independent Clause Test").

TEACHING SUGGESTION

Truths about Dependent Clauses [Text, 313–17]: Truths A and C serve as review. Truths B, D, and E are key components of this chapter. They are intended to assist students in their understanding of the roles not only of dependent clauses but also of the words that introduce them.

ALTERNATIVE "EXAMPLES"

Again, here is alternative wording for some of the example material in the text. It can help you introduce the material in a way that is different from the book's.

PAGES	HEADING	EXAMPLES AS IN BOOK	ALTERNATIVE EXAMPLES
314	**Truth A**	*I can tell that you will succeed.* *Students learn best when they study right.* *Students should know the times when they study best.*	***A dog can sense when he will undergo no harm.*** ***Exams go best when we have studied everything well.*** ***Students can learn the clues that something important is being said.***

PAGES	HEADING	EXAMPLES AS IN BOOK	ALTERNATIVE EXAMPLES
315	Truth C	*The birds knew that spring was near.* *The birds that we heard had just arrived.*	***The secretary knew that the call was important.*** ***The secretary that he hired works efficiently.***
316	Subord-inating Conjunc-tions	*We must finish this before the bus-es leave.*	***We stayed until the sun set.***
316-17	Question Words	*We asked what kind of bread was the most wholesome.*	***We found what kind of knot would be best.***
317	Truth D	*We finished the dishes before the evening news started.* *We knew that he would be late.*	***Gentlemen would go through a door after the lady went through.*** ***He thought that his answer was right.***
318-19	Truth E	*I remember who is coming.* *I remember whom I have phoned.* *I remember whose book I have borrowed.* *I remember whom I sent it to.* *I remember to whom I sent it.* *I remember where I have put my watch.*	***I know who the Presidents were.*** ***I know whom we should elect.*** ***I know whose answer is better.*** ***I know whom I should mail it to.*** ***I know to whom I should mail it.*** ***I know where the best hiding place is.***
321-23	Truth F	*He could not remember the road which he should be taking.* *The Scouts would remember the places where they could rest.* *He should be taking a road.* *He could not remember the road.* *The Scouts could rest at places.* *They would remember the places.*	***He would not forget the words which he had memorized.*** ***Some students will remember the page where they saw infor-mation.*** ***He memorized the words.*** ***He could not forget the words.*** ***Some students saw information.*** ***They will remember the page.***
324	Endnote: *That* & Adjec-tive Clauses	*I do not remember the day that you mentioned.*	***He needed the box that he had left behind.***
325	Endnote: *That* & Noun Clauses	*I know that you will do well.*	***I know that I should speak more distinctly.***

PAGES	HEADING	EXAMPLES AS IN BOOK	ALTERNATIVE EXAMPLES
325	**Endnote:** ***Whether***	*He did not say whether he would join us.*	***We are debating whether we should postpone the match.***

COMMENT ON THE "ENDNOTES" SECTION [Text, 96–97]

These endnotes supply important insights into how English works.

COMMENTS ON THE "REVIEW" SECTION [Text, 60]

Students should be able to write out (in their own words where appropriate) the new order of the TESTS and the STEPS of the Dependent Clause Test. They should have learned, by experience, that all the words of a clause—as a unit—do the job of a noun, adjective, or adverb. They must now recognize on sight all the introducers of dependent clauses that are emphasized in this chapter: namely, *that,* the nine subordinating conjunctions listed, and the nine question-word questions.

FINAL TEST

1. LIST ALL THE TESTS—IN CORRECT ORDER.
2. LIST THE STEPS OF THE DEPENDENT CLAUSE TEST AND IN ORDER.
3. LIST ANY TEN INTRODUCERS OF CLAUSES. For bonus credit: add nine more.
4. There are two kinds of introducers of clauses. EXPLAIN WHAT MAKES THEM DIFFERENT.
5. EXPLAIN WHY WE DO **NOT** NEED TO MARK A NOUN CLAUSE WITH THE LETTERING *N*.
6. EXPLAIN WHERE YOU FIND ADJECTIVE CLAUSES.
7. For the passage below, CARRY OUT ALL OF THE TESTS TO FOLLOW TO SUCCEED—AND IN THE RIGHT ORDER.

THANKSGIVING VACATION

If a daughter goes to college in a faraway city, problems arise when vacation time comes. For example, she will need a ride at Thanksgiving time.

For how many hours will people drive before they decide that the trip exhausts them too much? If this daughter could only share a ride with some friend, a secret wish of these beleaguered parents would be realized. Maybe they must drive to some halfway point because their daughter could not do better. Nonetheless, there is still hope that a better ride might materialize for the return trip.

ANSWERS FOR THE FINAL TEST

1. Comma Test, Main Subject Test—for Questions, Helpers plus WHAT/ING Word Verb Test, Do/does/did Test, Movable Starter Test, Main Subject Test—for Statements, Noun Job Tests, Dependent Clause Test, Adjective Test, Adverb Test
2. Label the clause introducer; place an opening side bracket before its first word; place a closing side bracket after its last word.
3. *that, before, after, though, although, until, while, if, because, since, how, when, where, why, who, whose, whom, which, what*
4. One kind does the job of introducer of the clause alone; the other does two jobs simultaneously—the job of introducer of the clause and the job that it performs inside

the clause (because it is a part of it).

5. A noun clause fills a noun-job territory; therefore, you mark it as doing the job of a noun as soon as you put an overhead bracket over it and label it as main subject, subject, object of verb, or object of preposition.

6. An adjective clause stands right after a noun or pronoun that is inside of a noun-job territory (and, therefore, under an overhead bracket that has the labeling circled-*S*, *S*, *OV*, or *OP*).

7. ⟨[If a daughter goes to college in a faraway city,]⟩ problems arise [when vacation time comes.] ⟨For example,⟩ she will need a ride at Thanksgiving time.

⟨For how many hours⟩ will people drive [before they decide [that the trip exhausts them too much]]?

⟨[If this daughter could only share a ride with some friend,]⟩ a secret wish of these beleaguered parents would be realized. ⟨Maybe⟩ they must drive to some halfway point [because their daughter could not do better.]

⟨Nonetheless,⟩ there is still hope [that a better ride might materialize for the return trip].

[Note how the question-word wording *For how many hours* has been correctly labeled "ADV" (for "adverb") and NOT "FAV" (for "front adverbial").]

Possible Weighting of Answers for the Final Test

1. 9% (4½% or ½ each for inclusion of all the tests and 4½% or ½ each for listing them in correct order).
2. 5% (1% each for including the step and 1% for place the remaining two in correct order).
3. 5% (½% for each correct answer).
4. 4% (2% for each correct answer).
5. 2%.
6. 2%.
7. 73% (.453 for each correct answer; there are 161 answers).

Appendix A

Rules for Agreement of a Verb with Its Subject

Objectives (Items in bolder letters are of greatest importance)

TO LEARN THESE RULES SO AS TO BE ABLE TO **SAY THEM IN ONE'S OWN WORDS**

Teaching Helps

NOTES REGARDING THE CHAPTERS AT WHICH THESE RULES SHOULD BE INTRODUCED

Rule for Keywords: This rule [Text, 327] presupposes instruction through Chapter 15, where KEYWORDS are explained.

Rule for Subjects That Follow Space-filler *There:* This rule [Text, 327–38] presupposes instruction through Chapter 9, where the term SPACE-FILLER *THERE* is explained.

Rule for a Few Indefinite Pronouns: This rule [Text, 328] presupposes instruction through Chapter 2, where the ONE/THING/BODY GROUP OF PRONOUNS are taught.

Rule for Subjects Modified by Prepositional Phrases: This rule [Text, 328-29] presupposes instruction through Chapter 15, where KEYWORDS are explained.

Rule for Subjects Joined by *And:* This rule [Text, 329] presupposes instruction through Chapter 12, where CONJUNCTIONS are taught.

Rule for Subjects Joined by *Or, Either ... Or,* or *Neither ... Nor:* This rule [Text, 329] presupposes instruction through Chapter 15, where KEYWORDS are explained.

ALTERNATIVE "EXAMPLES"

Again, here is alternative wording for some of the example material in the text. It can help you introduce the material in a way that is different from the book's.

PAGES	HEADING	EXAMPLES AS IN BOOK	ALTERNATIVE EXAMPLES
328	**Rule for Indefinite Pronouns**	*Everyone has worked hard.* *Everybody wants second helpings.* *Each of us knows what to do.* *Everybody has raised his / her hand.*	***Everyone has an equal chance.*** ***Everybody is prepared.*** ***Each of us has a job to do.*** ***Everybody has spoken his/her mind.***
328–29	**Rule for Subjects Modified by Prepositional Phrases**	*The reasons for that decision were convincing.* *The guide for the hikers has chosen a difficult trail.*	***The leaves on an oak tree change color later.*** ***The vote of a teenager counts the same as the vote of an adult.***

PAGES	HEADING	EXAMPLES AS IN BOOK	ALTERNATIVE EXAMPLES
329	**Rule for Subjects Joined by *And***	*Trees and shrubs add value to a person's property.* *Bill, Joan, and I are in the band.*	***Leaves and pine needles clutter a gutter.*** ***Tony, Joe, and Phil are my brothers.***
329	**Rule for Subjects Joined by *Or*, *Either ... Or*, or *Neither ... Nor***	*Light snow or flurries are predicted.* *Either Pedro or two of his friends are coming.* *Mice or a deer has ruined that tree.*	***Pencils or a pen is needed for the test.*** ***Either the carpenter or his helpers are coming to do the job.*** ***Cavities or gingivitis causes tooth decay.***

FINAL TEST

DIRECTIONS: For each of these sentences, circle the word that provides correct agreement of the verb with its subject.

1. Neither of the cars (is, are) dirty.
2. The girls and their brother (has, have) left already.
3. The bike of the Ritters (is, are) too unmanageable.
4. Everyone from our class (was, were) willing to help.
5. Neither his friends nor he (has, have) ever owned a camcorder.
6. There (is, are) several reasons for volunteering to help.
7. Each of these snowflakes (is, are) unique.
8. My chances for a quick win (is, are) slim.
9. The pitcher or its contents (is, are) responsible for the stain.
10. There (was, were) enough cookies for everyone.

USABLE AFTER CHAPTER 17

11. The answers that Fred put on his paper (was, were) carefully checked.
12. The proof that the area has mice (is, are) the loss of bark on the trunks of trees.

ANSWERS FOR THE FINAL TEST

1. Neither of the cars (**IS**, are) dirty.
2. The girls and their brother (has, **HAVE**) left already.
3. The bike of the Ritters (**IS**, are) too unmanageable.
4. Everyone from our class (**WAS**, were) willing to help.
5. Neither his friends nor he (**HAS**, have) ever owned a camcorder.
6. There (is, **ARE**) several reasons for volunteering to help.
7. Each of these snowflakes (**IS**, are) unique.
8. My chances for a quick win (is, **ARE**) slim.
9. The pitcher or its contents (is, **ARE**) responsible for the stain.
10. There (was, **WERE**) enough cookies for everyone.

USABLE AFTER CHAPTER 17

11. The answers that Fred put on his paper (was, **WERE**) carefully checked.
12. The proof that the area has mice (**IS**, are) the loss of bark on the trunks of trees.

POSSIBLE WEIGHTING OF ANSWERS FOR THE FINAL TEST: 10% each (or 8.3% each).

Copies of this text *The Hunter Writing System: Sentence Sense, Red Level* and the companion *Skills Practice Book, Answer Book,* and *Teacher's Guide* are available from the publisher:

Hunter & Joyce Publishing Company
R.R. 2, Box 54
Delhi, NY 13753

607-746-3196 · **800-462-7483** · Fax: 607-746-2408